"In *Breakfast with Bonhoeffer*, Jon Walker personally invites us into the telling story of God moving him from facts to faith, from truth to trust, from seeing 'with' to seeing 'through.' With the single eye of faith, Jon candidly testifies that on our journey into Christ-likeness, God directs us to his Kingdom reality through the rugged circumstances of life—the life we are currently in! This book is a provocative but productive read for all who may struggle to believe that God is wasting nothing in order to bring us into the family likeness. Highly recommended!"

—Steve Pettit, director, One in Christ; pastor, CenterPoint Christian Fellowship

"I love the writing style of Jon Walker. Like a master chef prepares an exquisite dining experience, Jon weaves words into pictures that evoke emotions long forgotten and spins new dreams and fresh possibilities that the reader somehow knows can become realities. He draws the reader in with his transparency and authenticity and, at the same time, challenges us to step out in faith, frail though it may be, knowing God will meet us there—at the point of our greatest need. *Breakfast with Bonhoeffer* is a must read for every heart longing to find fresh hope and renew their commitment to God."

—Mary Southerland, author, speaker, and co-founder of Girlfriends in God and Journey Ministry; www.marysoutherland.com

"Jon Walker takes Bonhoeffer's words and seamlessly applies them to his own set of life's problems. Jon's transparency and reliance on the Lord makes *Breakfast with Bonhoeffer* a book many can relate to today."

—Harold Harper, co-host, For Faith & Family Radio; author of *Josiah Road*

"I don't know when I have read such raw, powerful stories filled with such profound, real-life spiritual insight. PollyAnna Christians will be uncomfortable with Jon's candor about his struggles, but the truth is, as the Psalmist says, that the Lord's table is spread for us in the presence of our enemies. The greatest treasures in Christ are gained by those who persevere through the most dire tribulation. In these pages, Jon shares the treasure he has found."

—Mark Kelly, editor and publisher, MultiplyJustice.net

"Powerful and painfully honest, Jon Walker's storytelling is pitch perfect. Tempered with truth and humor, it is a poignant reminder that God's providence does not always come wrapped in the packaging we expect. Ultimately, *Breakfast with Bonhoeffer* is not just a book about the bloody battle of love and sorrow that is sometimes life here in the in-between; it's a melodious song of a fragile human being who learns to sing and trust in spite of anxiety and circumstances."

—Kathy Chapman Sharp, author of *Life's Too Short to Miss the Big Picture for Women*

"With brutal honesty, Jon Walker invites us on a deeply personal exploration of Bonhoeffer's call for radical discipleship. The truths contain the grit and glory of the human experience through the lens of Bonhoeffer's timeless writings and Walker's contemporary narrative."

—Matt Tullos, senior pastor, Bluegrass Baptist Church, Hendersonville, Tennessee

BREAKFAST *with* BONHOEFFER

BREAKFAST *with*
BONHOEFFER

HOW I LEARNED TO STOP BEING RELIGIOUS SO I COULD FOLLOW JESUS

JON WALKER

LEAFWOOD
PUBLISHERS

BREAKFAST WITH BONHOEFFER

HOW I LEARNED TO STOP BEING RELIGIOUS SO I COULD FOLLOW JESUS

Copyright 2012 by Jon Walker

ISBN 978-0-89112-340-8

Printed in the United States of America

Cover design by Thinkpen Design, LLC
Interior text design by Sandy Armstrong

Leafwood Publishers
1626 Campus Court
Abilene, Texas 79601
1-877-816-4455 toll free

For current information about all Leafwood titles, visit our website:
www.leafwoodpublishers.com

12 13 14 15 16 17 / 7 6 5 4 3

To Sherry, with love

ACKNOWLEDGEMENTS

It is impossible to write a book without admitting, like Tennyson, "I am part of all that I have met." That being the case, it is beyond my abilities to thank everyone who helped me while writing this book, but I do want to mention the extraordinary patience of Leonard Allen and Gary Myers plus the unselfish support of Susan and David Moffitt, Allison Cox, Mark Kelly, Kelly Sims, Harold Harper, Lori Hensley, Kathy Chapman Sharp, Donna Stetzer, Grace Guthrie, Doug Hart, Steve Pettit, Matt Tullos, Erich Bridges, Katie and Cleve Persinger, Carolyn Baker, Billy and Whitney Hensley, Tobin Perry, Brandon Cox, Terry Whaley, Jordan Camenker, Kim Glaner, Rick Warren, David Chrzan, Anne Krumm, Robert Supernor, Nicole Knox, Andrew Accardy, Sally Killian, Laura Vest, Christopher Walker, Nathan Walker, and Jasmine.

CONTENTS

INTRODUCTION

Several years ago, in one of those God-things, my friend Bucky Rosenbaum introduced me to Gary Myers and Leonard Allen from Leafwood Publishers. They were looking for a writer familiar with Dietrich Bonhoeffer who could teach his concepts of costly grace to a new generation.

It proved to be a good match and, for reasons this book will explain, a project that God used to strengthen me even as he sifted me during a very challenging year. The result of that meeting was the book, *Costly Grace*.

While writing *Costly Grace*, I would take my dog for walks each morning and, in a sense, have conversations with Bonhoeffer as I tried to understand his beliefs on the cost of grace, the need for a concrete faith, and the critical nature of keeping our walk centered exclusively on Christ. During those walks, I saw how easily his practical, hands-on theology fit into my own circumstances, but I also found myself arguing with Bonhoeffer—and ultimately Jesus—over some of the hard truths involved in following Christ.

Gary and I discussed those conversations, and he suggested I write a more personal book about the things I learned from Bonhoeffer. You're now holding that book in your hands. You'll understand why this was a difficult book to write, and so I think it is important to explain my approach to this very personal story.

First, writers are always required to make choices about what to put in and what to leave out, what best tells the story and what will become a distraction to the reader. In writing this narrative, I clearly do not tell everything or get into considerable detail. I chose to do this because I wanted to be as fair and even-handed as possible in such a narrative.

There is no need to go into such detail in order to tell my story, which is about God's faithful involvement in our considerably flawed lives. In writing this narrative, I was reminded of the sin, past and present, in my life and the need to extend grace just as I accept grace.

Second, this narrative exposes a messy faith, but I intended it that way. I know mine has been messy over the years, and I know many loving, committed believers who continue to grow and mature because they keep following Jesus, despite their messy faith.

I look in the Bible and I see messy faith in both the Old and New Testaments. Many of the biblical lessons that teach us about faith emerge from the messy faith of the disciples.

Dietrich Bonhoeffer lived a messy faith, believing Jesus continually brings us to choices that require total dependence upon him in order to take the next step. This means we stop being afraid of making mistakes, trusting that, if we mis-step, God sweeps in with his grace, is faithful to forgive, and will work things out to get us back on track because he wants us to move forward in our journey. Bonhoeffer teaches that a life of such extraordinary risk is the *expectation*, not the exception, for any disciple of Jesus.

"This is the world, as best as I can remember it."

—Rich Mullins

chapter 1

ZILLOW DREAMS

At night I chase Zillow dreams that stretch across a pixeled landscape. I'm trying to get back, looking for a way to slip into the promised land as quickly as I'd slipped out. I long to return home.

Perhaps I should explain that Zillow is a real estate app that offers a map of all the neighborhoods and streets in your town. Type in a ZIP code and you're given a satellite view showing all the houses for sale in that area. Click on a house for sale, and you can see pictures and information about each little parcel of the American Dream. The promised land. The place I call home.

Wrapped in the neon glow of my iPad, I virtually walk the streets of my town, stopping to look at homes I once could afford, lingering to think of what it might be like to live in that house or this one, seeing my sons running up the stairs to the bonus room we'd promised, seeing them climbing up the jungle gym we swore would be part of the backyard.

Like Peter Pan, I can fly to another street, another house, and imagine looking in on Wendy and the boys all snuggled in safe for the night, under the watchful eye of the family dog. I walk past houses that I once couldn't afford, that I might could if I still had a down payment, if I still had a job.

Even if I could get back all the money we lost, all the equity swept away by the wind of economic crisis, I don't think I'd buy a new home, because I am no longer confident the value of any home is stable. Most of all, for the first time in my life, I'm afraid—afraid that I can no longer consistently make the income to keep paying a mortgage every month.

> . . . following Jesus means that "the disciple is dragged out of his relative security into a life of absolute insecurity (that is, in truth, into the absolute security and safety of the fellowship of Jesus)."

Every day I am discipled by Dietrich Bonhoeffer, as I work on a book related to his classic, *The Cost of Discipleship*, one of the most influential books of the twentieth century. Bonhoeffer writes when Germany is under Nazi rule, moving quickly and steadily toward world war. He sees the instability of the economy and the government, as well as the church in Germany compromising in order to retain its power and position. In 1933, as a young pastor, Bonhoeffer takes a public stand against Hitler, telling the German people that their worship of the Führer was nothing less than idolatry and that their number one focus should be on the Kingdom of Heaven, not the economic relief they still desperately needed following World War I.

Bonhoeffer knows that restoring hope to the German people requires an intimate relationship with Christ; the government could not provide anything more than temporary hope and unstable solutions. He taught the truth that real stability can only be found with Jesus.

Bonhoeffer says following Jesus means that "the disciple is dragged out of his relative security into a life of absolute insecurity (that is, in truth, into the absolute security and safety of the fellowship of Jesus), from a life which is observable and calculable (it is, in fact, quite incalculable) into a life where everything is unobservable and fortuitous (that is, into one which is necessary and calculable), out of the realm of finite (which is in truth the infinite) into the realm of infinite possibilities (which is the one liberating reality)."

Bonhoeffer speaks about the reality of the Kingdom of Heaven, that through grace we are able to follow Jesus into a new land. We follow him into the Kingdom, and there we learn to live according to the rules and laws established by our King. We live as citizens of that world and not this world.

But the Kingdom is not in a far and distant future. It is also a place that we can enter now through faith in Jesus. But to enter the Kingdom, we must *comprehensively* and *absolutely* walk away from the way we do life now so we can follow Jesus down an *exclusive* path through *the* narrow gate that leads to the Kingdom.

Is it possible that by chasing Zillow dreams, I'm focusing on getting back to the wrong place? Have I replaced the Kingdom of Heaven with the deceptive glow of the American dream?

Do I live in the world's economy or in God's economy? Do I believe it's all up to me to pay for things and to provide for my family? Do I believe it's up to the government?

Or do I believe in God's economy, that our Father is the provider, and he knows our needs better than we do ourselves? If he knows when a sparrow falls, does he know that I'm without a job again? Does he know that all the money is gone?

Bonhoeffer says, "It is senseless to pretend that we can make provision because we cannot alter the circumstances of this world. Only God can take care, for it is he who rules the world. Since we cannot take care, since we are so completely powerless, we ought not to do it either. If we do, we are dethroning God and presuming to rule the world ourselves."

Since we cannot even predict what will happen tomorrow, how great is our arrogance to believe we can maneuver an economic crisis without God? Are we petty, little lords, incapable of controlling the future or even our present circumstances but still wrestling to take control from our Creator, who says he will fulfill our every need?

——— ——

Yet the longing I feel is toward Zillow dreams, not the Kingdom, as if life consists of living in a home. Even though I've just seen the American dream turn into a nightmare on Suburban Street, the house is the hardest dream to give up. You wish for the stability of your children growing up in a home in a safe neighborhood, near good schools that lead to best friends and prom dates, for the boys coming home and playing football in the backyard and Nerf combat in the living room. A barbecue on the back porch. The white picket fence.

> "Only God can take care, for it is he who rules the world. Since we cannot take care, since we are so completely powerless, we ought not to do it either. If we do, we are dethroning God and presuming to rule the world ourselves."
>
> —BONHOEFFER

Are these an essential part of the abundant life? Am I willing to serve Jesus, but only within the context of the American dream? Am I willing to serve Jesus, but only as long as my kids can live a normal life as defined by the American dream?

I think about how deeply rooted the dream is, because I never even liked the suburban jungle and high school, where everyone gets pushed into pageants of who's normal and who's nerd.

In Kingdom living, is it possible God knows the very place that will help my sons grow spiritually and become everything he created them to be, whether that's a house, an apartment, or a hut? Bonhoeffer says the disciples left everything behind in order to follow, believing that the promises of Jesus provided greater security "than all the securities in the world."

He says when we focus on anything other than Jesus, we're looking at a mirage of the real world. We're simply trafficking in shadows that shift and slip away without warning. By focusing on Christ, we catch a glimpse of the real world established in the Kingdom of Heaven.

——— ——

I think about how much money we lost when we were forced to sell our home just as the bottom dropped out of the housing market. You read about the housing crisis, but the numbers are abstract symbols, never revealing the heartache of losing your family's home, never revealing the effect it has on your children and on your own psyche.

I never thought I would come to a place where I could no longer pay for my home. I never thought I'd lose confidence that I could make enough money to pay for my home. I never thought I'd lose my home.

We bought our first home by cashing out a small retirement plan and using it for a down payment, believing it was a necessary sacrifice so that our sons could grow up in a house. Now they live in a cramped apartment.

The equity we lost when we sold the home represented a lifetime of savings and extra work, years of extra jobs, overtime, settling for "new" furniture from yard sales, and vacationing wherever family members happened to live. I used to joke, "I wish someone in the family would move, so we could see a different city this summer."

We regularly paid extra on our mortgage in hopes of paying it off sooner than later, and we did that by remaining debt free except for the mortgage and one car payment.

We always made our mortgage payments on time. We had excellent credit, but then we hit a financial crisis brought on by a perfect storm of a lay-off, an overpriced housing market, the problems with the economy, and, yes, some lack of planning on our part.

I tried to refinance the house but couldn't get a rate that would lower the mortgage payments enough to make it worthwhile. I tried to convince the mortgage company to lower my rate enough so I could handle the payments, but they wouldn't budge. Shortly after I sold the house at a price that wiped out all our equity, the mortgage companies started offering lower rates in hopes of forestalling defaults.

Within two years, the rates dropped so drastically that, if we still owned the home, we could have refinanced into an affordable monthly payment and kept the house. When I was waiting for the house to sell and uncertain if I could make the next month's payment, I called the mortgage company to explore my options. There were none. If I failed to make my payment for a few months, then they had a default department that could talk to me about my options.

The economic recovery plan included a program to help people in my situation, so I checked into that. I was asked if I had more than $6,800 in cash, stocks, bonds, CDs—anything that could be liquidated. "Yes, I have $10,000, but that is all I have left. Period. And since I am trying to make a living as an independent contractor, a significant portion of that money is set aside to pay my taxes. And I also have to eat."

But until I had less than $6,800, I wouldn't qualify. I said, "That's not really a mortgage assistance plan; that's designed to have me pay out until I'm out of money, and then you'll help me so I won't default."

> "Here is the sum of the commandments—
> to live in fellowship with Christ."
>
> —BONHOEFFER

In addition, once the government helped me get into a payment I could handle, they would own a portion of my home, and I would have to share any profit I made when I sold the home—up to 50 percent. I didn't like the idea of the government having its hands in my home, so I dismissed that idea.

Bonhoeffer says our only hope to enter the Kingdom of Heaven lies with Jesus Christ. But he won't allow us to see eternal life as a distant dream; he insists we follow him into that life now: *The Kingdom of Heaven is upon you.*

"Here is the sum of the commandments—to live in fellowship with Christ," says Bonhoeffer. Jesus must bring us to the place where we abandon anything that holds us to the old life, anything that distracts us from the Kingdom of Heaven.

After the house sold and we lost nearly everything we had in it, I remember thinking, "If I had known I was going to lose all this money, I would have given it to the church." Right then, Jesus tapped me on the shoulder and said, "Did you even bother to ask if that's what I wanted you to do in the first place?"

I know now I have to abandon my Zillow dream, but of all the things I lost or will soon lose, this is the hardest dream to give up, because I had a deeply rooted desire to see my sons grow up in a home of our own.

If I'd known how difficult and costly the journey would become, I would have tried to drop out—but, then again, there was no other option left. I had no other choice.

This, then, is the story of how I died.

chapter 2

DOUBLE VISION

The windows in our living room are floor-to-ceiling, wall-to-wall, meant to give the sense of openness, inviting light, with a tremendous view of the backyard. If this house could be transported to our lot in California, it would be an impressive view of the American Dream.

God blessed us with one of the largest lots in Mission Viejo, Calif., one that included a pool and palm trees, a playhouse and jungle gym play-set, and yet still enough room for a condo-sized stretch of grass, all backing up to a huge berm that put our back-door neighbor perhaps ten feet above us, creating the illusion of privacy.

Every day after school, my youngest son would head straight for the jungle gym, where you could see him acting out the adventures most of us have when we're young, the kind of dreams where the hero never losses and the crisis always deals with such persistent problems as a supervillian trying to take over the city or releasing a dirty bomb during the World Series. The hero never faces off against the more monstrous and diabolical villains such as a crumbling economy or an agonizing divorce.

In Southern California, with its year-round comfortable climate, a backyard is like another room in the house. Sometimes, after dinner on the porch, we'd take dinner guests and climb to the top of the berm, and there we'd sit looking out across our pool and over the top of our house at miles and miles of Southern California scenery. We joked about turning the berm into an amphitheater by dropping a screen from the roof of the house and projecting movies under the California stars.

As the crow flies under those stars, it was about seven miles to Laguna Beach, where The Beach Boys went on a surfin' safari. Jump on the 5 heading south and you can catch a wave at Doheny, too. Head north, and you're cruising toward Disneyland, L.A., swimming pools, movie stars. Y'all come back now.

This is where Rick Warren sat on a beach, watching surfers catch a wave to ride it into shore. This is where God showed him that, in ministry, you don't have to build the wave—that's God's job. You just need to see where God is working, where the wave is building, and join God in his work.

Sensing God's call to Saddleback Church, my family left Nashville just as Katrina hit landfall in New Orleans. The torrential rains reached far enough north that I was soaked to the skin after loading the car, so I had to change my clothes before we left. My wife and youngest son flew, but I was driving across country in my PT Cruiser. My traveling companion was nine years old, and we were heading toward Memphis and Graceland.

We drove across America in the summer heat, listening to an iPod instead of the radio, so we were marginally aware of the devastation in New Orleans—the city underwater, the homeless waiting for busses by the side of the road, an abrupt and bleak community displaced in the Super Dome.

We journeyed through the heartland, where the buffalo once roamed, for a while joining Nat King Cole on Route 66: Oklahoma City, Amarillo and Gallup, New Mexico. It brought back memories of summer vacations when I was a boy, sitting in the backseat with my sister looking for the night's motel, preferably one with a pool and a bed that would vibrate when you dropped a quarter in the slot. (Do we look back at what was real or what was ideal?)

My son played "Cheeseburger in Paradise" 291 times on the iPod. As we'd pull away from one set of gas pumps, I told my son that we used to call them service stations because an attendant pumped your gas, checked your oil, and washed your windows, *and* they only charged you 30 cents a gallon. And every time we'd stop for gas, I felt a little tug in my stomach, because every day, as we crossed the heartland and the badlands, the prices went up.

My son and I pushed on, cruising across the deserts and mountain ranges that our forefathers crossed in wagon trains as they looked for a place to put down roots and live the American Dream. They wanted freedom and at least a chance to let their hard work and sacrifice pay off for them and their children.

We pressed on into the cultural promised land of California, where people bring their dreams of wealth and fame, where we package the dream and sell it on screens across the world. Our final destination was Mission Viejo, an older community in Orange County just a few miles from Saddleback.

But this floor-to-ceiling, wall-to-wall windowed house is not on our idyllic California lot; it is the home we foolishly bought after returning to Nashville. We bought it based on a contract I had with a company in California, and then within a week of the closing, the company laid everyone off.

The backyard to this house is empty, the lay-off stealing the promised playset for my youngest son. I remember that with every house we considered, he'd run straight to the back-yard and judge the house according to whether the backyard could help generate his dreams and adventures.

My view through those floor-to-ceiling, wall-to-wall win-dows is overcast and gloomy, and the empty lots that run down the street behind us are full of weeds and rocks. This is bad land. Hard and rocky, it's a major ordeal just to plant a tree and, as a result, it was never farmland. Instead, it was used for an inter-national steeple chase with hills, ditches, and rough terrain on a challenging cross-country course, back before the race was manicured into the fence and track run we know today.

There are a few houses scattered here and there in the neighborhood, many of them sitting empty because nothing is selling. Some are half built, construction stopped because the economy is faltering and the market on all these over-priced homes is collapsing. One house sits at the top of the hill like a creepy, ghostly mansion backlit by lightning on a dark and rainy night. The unfinished house has a cracked foundation and a broken skylight that summons rain into the kitchen to splash across the cabinets and neglected stovetop.

> Following Jesus down the narrow path
> and through the narrow gate into the
> Kingdom of Heaven with double vision is
> more difficult than a drunk trying to stay
> steady and straight while touching his
> nose or walking heel-to-toe down the line.

It's not just in my neighborhood; you can drive up and down the major thoroughfare a few blocks from my house and see neighborhood after neighborhood overrun by "For Sale" signs. Nobody wants to buy.

———— ——

Most of us try to live with one eye on Jesus and one eye on the world. The only thing that does is give us double vision. Following Jesus down the narrow path and through the narrow gate into the Kingdom of Heaven with double vision is more difficult than a drunk trying to stay steady and straight while touching his nose or walking heel-to-toe down the line.

Every step is unstable and unsure. Everything you see is skewed by two images, neither one representing the exact likeness of that at which you are looking. I know this difficulty of double vision. I've had it ever since the football was high and to the right, leaving me stretched vulnerably in the air. The linebacker swept his forearm through the ball, unintentionally using his elbow like a pile driver smashing through my glasses and driving them into the bottom ridge of my right eye socket.

Once I was on my feet, the horizon shifted to the right and then to the left like it was sitting on a teeter-totter. Walking toward the sidelines, I was like a boat being pushed off target by the current, steadily drifting to the left.

There was a jagged cut across the eyelid and a deep cut under my eye, but the doctor also found slivers of glass lodged in the eyeball. He said I was fortunate because the glass was only in the white of the eye, so there was no damage to the cornea. He meticulously removed the glass in my eye and then used around forty-five stitches to sew up the cuts.

The doctor used a local anesthesia, so as I lay there, I watched him bring the needle down, then I could feel that unsettling tug that comes when thread is pulled through your skin, then I watched as he pulled the needle back up and then started down again. Wash. Rinse. Repeat. My mother tried to hold my hand, but I pushed her away. I could handle this on my own—an attitude that would eventually lead to my death.

The doctor did an extraordinary job; the scars were hardly noticeable. But the muscle under my right eye was permanently weakened, so it tilts up ever so slightly. If you look into my eyes, you can't see the tilt, but it's just enough to keep my eyes from lining up together in coordinated vision. I've had this double vision since junior high.

You can imagine how disorienting life can be when there's always a double-image of the things you see. Imagine driving. Imagine trying to pour yourself a glass of tea. Imagine trying to read. Imagine talking to someone when a second image of their face is slightly up and to the right of the first image. It can drive you crazy, not to mention give you a huge, daylong headache.

This is how so many of us try to follow Jesus. We keep one eye on the world and the other on the Kingdom—and that skews everything we see. Our focus is constantly shifting from one image to the other. We stumble along, trying to walk a straight line but instead staggering between what is right and what we think is right. And we call this normal; we call this discipleship.

I think about this when Bonhoeffer says we should have a singular focus on Jesus. We were never meant to walk with double vision, and seeing double doesn't give you a double-focus because—this I know well—you can't focus on anything when you're seeing more than one image. By its very nature, double vision is unfocused.

A few weeks after the accident to my eye, I began to have single vision again—not because my right eye healed and re-aligned with the left, but because my brain could not keep processing the two images.

To this day, when I open my eyes each morning, I still see double for a few seconds, and then the image coming from my left eye fades away like a scene dissolving in a movie, leaving me with single vision coming from my dominate right eye. My brain made a choice between the two masters. But get this: My right eye is the damaged eye.

When we aren't intentional on seeing the whole of reality through the eyes of Jesus, we most likely will default into a damaged view of the world.

> "From the human point of view everything looks hopeless, but Jesus sees things with different eyes. Instead of the people maltreated, wretched and poor, he sees the ripe harvest field of God."
>
> —BONHOEFFER

Since the accident, I've worn corrective glasses that have a prism ground into each lens. The prisms force my eyes to re-align so that I see normally with both eyes. This is an image of what Jesus does when he gives us his eyes, when he shows us how citizens of the Kingdom are able to see. You could say the Jesus-prism adjusts our vision so that we can see the whole of reality. We can see the Kingdom truth that all things come from Jesus, go through Jesus, and come back to Jesus (Romans 11:36).

"From the human point of view everything looks hopeless, but Jesus sees things with different eyes," says Bonhoeffer. "Instead of the people maltreated, wretched and poor, he sees the ripe harvest field of God. The hour has come for these poor and wretched folk to be fetched home to the kingdom of God."

The lens of Jesus shows us that people before us are not our enemy; rather, they, like we once were, are lost in the enemy's dark kingdom, and we offer the light they need to find their way to Jesus.

Jesus tells us again and again that we have to
things of this world into the eternal reality of t
When people approached him to tell him about their circumstances, he'd say something like, "You're looking for a drink
of water, but look past your circumstances, because I'm the
living water. I can quench your thirst for eternity, not just in
this moment. Can you see that Kingdom truth?"

Or, "You want to see bread right now, but I want you to
see that I am the living bread. I can feed you for this one meal,
but—Look!—I can feed you for all eternity if you'll put your
trust in me. Can you see that Kingdom truth?"

Paul says that in order to see like Jesus sees, we have to set
our eyes on eternity: "Don't shuffle along, eyes to the ground,
absorbed with the things right in front of you. Look up, and
be alert to what is going on around Christ—that's where the
action is. See things from his perspective" (Colossians 3:2 MSG).

Seeing Kingdom reality while living in this world is not
about alternating between two pairs of glasses as your circumstances change. It's more like wearing bifocals. I wear bifocals
because my lens correct so I can see far—into eternity. The
bifocal allows me to see what is up close while still looking
through the larger lens—the Jesus lens. I don't have one eye on
the world and one eye on the Kingdom. I have both eyes "fixed
on Jesus, on whom our faith depends from beginning to end"
(Hebrews 12:2 TEV).

chapter 3

DOUBLE-MINDED

When I look in the mirror, I don't recognize the man I see. I no longer need to lose just a few pounds. I'm not overweight. I'm not heavy-set. I'm obese, and I'm having trouble seeing what is obvious to anyone who looks at me.

The mirror shows me the deep bags under my eyes along with the double chins that round my face. My receding hairline has ebbed permanently to low tide. My beard, a statement of independence among clean-shaven, button-down preachers when I was younger, has steadily turned white, and now it just makes me look old.

I look like Santa must feel at 6 AM Polar time in December. Underneath the mess, I see an echo of my father's face, but my father, in his old age, never looked this bad.

The thing is, I walk away from the mirror, and I forget what I look like. Instead, the image in my head is of a younger man with brown hair, blue eyes, and a sardonic smile. I really should just lose a few pounds.

Without conscious thought, I keep that image of the younger man in my head, but, every once in a while, I'll pass a mirror or a glass door, and the truth materializes. I beat back the intrusion of reality by quickly walking away. Sometimes I think about the man described by James who looks in the mirror, but, when he walks away, forgets what he looks like.

His point is that when we listen to the Word, but do not do what it says, we are living a lie. We are denying reality, keeping it from penetrating our lives with truth.

Sometimes when my computer screen fades dark because I've been thinking too long about how to write a sentence, reality pushes through, revealing my reflection in the screen. There I am, staring at a true image of myself, and I quickly press a key to take me back to my delusions.

This morning Bonhoeffer reminds me that as long as we live with our delusions, we hinder ourselves from engaging the Kingdom of Heaven in the now. His father was a psychiatrist, so I know he has picked this word—delusions—quite deliberately.

We live with delusions that we control life, delusions that we can bring goodness to God and earn his favor, delusions that God can be compartmentalized into the convenient corners of our lives.

But Bonhoeffer tells me Jesus is intent on breaking through our delusions and forcing us to look at the reality of our sin, his grace, the world's decay, and the Kingdom of Heaven in our midst. He says, "The call of Jesus teaches us that our relation to the world has been built on an illusion. All the time we thought we had enjoyed a direct relation with men and things. This is what had hindered us from faith and obedience."

> Cheap grace "is the preaching of forgiveness without requiring repentance, baptism without church discipline, Communion without confession, absolution without personal confession. Cheap grace is grace without discipleship, grace without the cross, grace without Jesus Christ, living and incarnate."
> –BONHOEFFER

He says our faith must be real, not an intellectual assent where the forgiveness of sin is proclaimed as a general truth and the love of God taught as an abstract concept, where we agree there is a Supreme Being but deny the necessity of the Incarnation of God's Word.

This cheap grace, Bonhoeffer says, "is the preaching of forgiveness without requiring repentance, baptism without church discipline, Communion without confession, absolution without personal confession. Cheap grace is grace without discipleship, grace without the cross, grace without Jesus Christ, living and incarnate."

It is like an obese man denying the reality of calories and fat grams and carrying on his affair with Little Debbie.

Bonhoeffer also says our faith must be concrete. We must exercise our faith, taking the steps Jesus tells us to take when he tells us to take them. It is only by taking actual steps of faith that we can see Jesus is real and trustworthy. In other words, our faith will never increase simply by agreeing we need faith in Jesus; we must take what Bonhoeffer calls a concrete step— and not just any step, but only the ones Jesus tells us to take.

Otherwise, we're like an obese man who can understand the need to exercise, talk about exercise, and even plan to exercise, but who does not actually begin to exercise. It does him no good.

Is it possible we no longer live lives of faith because we've become fat on our religious traditions and addicted to our fast-food formulas that keep us at an arm's length from Jesus? Why do we ask what Jesus would do instead of asking Jesus what he wants us to do? In any other relationship, wouldn't that be a sign of dysfunction? Are we serving an abstract savior who forgives us of our abstract sins? Does that make us abstract Christians?

——— ——

I have a medical form of double-mindedness, more commonly called bipolar disorder. I wasn't diagnosed with the disease until I was forty-nine years old, but once the doctors figured it out, some of the problems I've experienced throughout my life suddenly made sense. And when I look back now, I see an instability that I'd never seen before. In fact, my self-image was entirely different—one of great stability. I mean, I was the "go to" guy. I was the one who put in the extra hours and made sure the job was done right. But this is the thing about bipolar disorder II: When I "swing up," my disorder shows up as high productivity and high energy. Nowadays, I joke that I need to plan my work around my upswings.

But I also seem powerless to dictate my own moods. Yes, we all wake up cranky in the morning, but sometimes I could feel something shifting in me when I was in the middle of a meeting. I'm not talking about getting angry or excited because of something someone says or does. It was more like when you go the ophthalmologist and she's flipping lenses, asking you how the shift of each lens affects your vision: "Is it A or is it B?"

It's sort of like that. I can be sitting at my desk, in a meeting, out to lunch—wherever—and something happens to rotate a lens, and straightway I see everything differently. It's like a veil of anxiety, detachment, or depression is pulled across my brain.

Other days, my thoughts start running like a chipmunk on caffeine: "Gotta finish that project. Should start with . . . grocery store! Milk . . . oh, that's the way to start that. But what was that about yesterday . . . milk, bread . . . article idea! Oh, even better one. Where's my pencil—is it in those boxes? Start cleaning out those boxes . . . no, wait, go to the grocery store. Whoa, I have to finish the project!"

Sometimes I can't turn it off. Creative ideas come through so quickly I can never get them all down, and, many times, when my thoughts are racing, I can't understand the notes I've made. Trivial thoughts will sweep in and I can't get off that track.

I can't get to sleep, because that chipmunk keeps speeding around that squeaky exercise wheel. One manifestation of this is that sometimes when I'm getting dressed, I put on a shirt, realize I have to check the calendar in the kitchen, come back to put on my socks, grab my toothbrush, remember I need my sweater, and then I find myself standing in front of the bathroom mirror brushing my teeth with only one arm in the shirt sleeve and partially through a jacket sleeve and only one sock on. I do not have ADHD, but bipolar II carries similar characteristics.

I can also get so fixated on one sequence of thought, going through it over and over again until it feels as if a rut is being burned in my brain. Some days I wake up with dry, tentative feeling, similar to a hangover, although I don't drink. In those moments, I can be agitated or animated, like a Starbucks junkie who hasn't had his first fix.

I sometimes wake up at night with what I can only describe as intense loneliness that almost takes on a physical form. It is like a black hole has opened in my head and the vast emptiness of space is being sucked into my brain.

One of the things I hate about bipolar disorder is that I can sometimes forget what I know. In other words, I have the answer; I have the plan; I know what I'm supposed to do, but then under stress that all disappears and I start trying to figure it out all over again.

This example is minor, but it remains in my memory. When I was in the second grade, we took a Christmas quiz with a number of fill-in-the-blank sentences attached to a set of words for finding the answers.

Once sentence was: "Reindeer are _____." I kept looking through the choices and couldn't find a correct answer.

So I settled on brown, even though that meant I was using the word twice. "Reindeer are brown."

By the way, this was in Kansas, so our math problems were like this: There are twenty-nine munchkins and one scarecrow in a ditch beside the Yellow Brick Road hunkered down against a tornado. When the storm twists through, it takes thirteen munchkins with it. How many munchkins are left beside the Yellow Brick Road?

Anyway, I took my test paper up to the teacher, and she told me I was wrong and that I had to re-do the test. I stood at her desk for a second and realized the correct word was "real." "Reindeer are real" (yes, go check it out—non-flying, non-brown caribou).

So I went back to my seat. By "re-do" the test, the teacher meant to start with a blank answer sheet and do it all over again. I went through the fill-in blanks, and when I got to reindeer, I was perplexed. I couldn't see the answer. I finally wrote down "brown" and took the test up to the teacher.

You know it: She told me I was wrong and that I had to re-do the test. Once again, I stood there looking at the blackboard until I realized the correct word was "real." How could I forget that? "Reindeer are real."

I went back to my seat. I re-did the test. I filled in the blank: "Reindeer are brown." I went to the teacher. She said go re-do the test. I looked at the blackboard. I remembered the answer was "real." You can imagine how idiotic I felt.

This time I went back to my seat and the first sentence I filled in was "Reindeer are real."

When we aren't focused on what is real—on Kingdom reality—it's like we have bipolar faith. We swing from belief to unbelief, from hot to cold without ever being either. Jesus says our lukewarm faith makes him want to puke (Revelation 3:15-18).

We start thinking like citizens of the Kingdom, but then we get lost in the maze of life, distracted by temporary things that seem so important in the moment. We understand our desperate situation and embrace God's grace, but then, like the Galatians, we slip back into our own way of thinking about what we must do to please God or what we must do just to survive until the weekend.

> When we aren't focused on what is real—on Kingdom reality—it's like we have bipolar faith. We swing from belief to unbelief, from hot to cold without ever being either. Jesus says our lukewarm faith makes him want to puke.

Peter shows the ups and downs of bipolar faith, something most of us experience as we struggle to change from fallen thinking to Kingdom thinking. We get it, then we don't, then we get it again.

Peter swears he'll die for Jesus, but then he swears he doesn't even know Jesus while warming his hands by a fire in the courtyard of the high priest's house (John 18:25-27). He takes a huge step of faith, walking on water, and then sinks beneath the waves by taking his focus off Jesus (Matthew 14:28-33).

There was one day when Peter saw clearly into the reality of the Kingdom. He and the other disciples were on their way to the villages near Caesarea Philippi, and Jesus asked them, "Tell me, who do people say I am?"

They talked about a variety of opinions. Some people thought he was John the Baptist, others Elijah or Jeremiah, and still others suggested he could be one of the other prophets.

"What about you?" Jesus asked. "Who do you say I am?"

Peter said, "You are the Messiah, the Son of the living God."

Jesus praised Peter, then said, "You didn't get that answer out of books or from teachers. My Father in heaven, God himself, let you in on this secret of who I really am."

But as Jesus began to tell the disciples that he must be sacrificed for the sins of the world, Peter pulled him aside and rebuked him: "This will never happen, Lord, as long as I'm beside you!"

Jesus responds: "Get away from me, Satan! You are an obstacle in my way, because these thoughts of yours don't come from God, but from human nature."

Peter was seeing things from a human perspective and disregarding God's point-of-view—Kingdom thinking versus faithless thinking. The strong rebuke from Jesus is because Peter's insistence is nothing short of an assault on God's sovereignty. In fact, if Peter succeeded in stopping Jesus, then Christ would never suffer on the cross (Mark 8:27-29, TEV; Matthew 16:17-19, MSG).

In the Sermon on the Mount, Jesus declares his followers citizens of the Kingdom, and then he outlines the shift we must make to Kingdom thinking:

"You are living in the far country, and I have come to bring you home to the Father. We have a difficult journey ahead of us, but I will be with you for every step, and as we journey, I want you to learn the ways of the Kingdom so you will be fully prepared as we enter the gates of Heaven.

It is critical that you learn to think like the Father, and that means you can no longer live with this delusion of self-righteousness. You have to stop thinking you can be good enough for God. Trust me, and I can guarantee you'll make it through the narrow gate.

And if you choose to follow me, this is what it will be like:

Dependent

You've been told to think that you can bring your goodness to God, but I've come to teach you that in the Kingdom of Heaven, God brings his goodness to you.

Mourning

You've been told to think that your security is in your jobs and homes and retirement accounts, but I've come to teach you that the world is spinning into disaster. Get your head into the Kingdom of Heaven, so you can see the world for what it is.

Meek

You've been told you must cling to your rights, but I've come to teach you to patiently endure, trusting with absolute certainty that our Father is looking out for you. Your rights may be taken away, but you can never be snatched from the Father's hand.

Just

You've been told to think you must demand justice now, but I've come to teach you that justice is part of my endgame. Justice will prevail in the Kingdom. So why waste time protecting temporary positions and possessions when there is so much to do to bring as many people as possible into the Kingdom?

Merciful

You've been told to think that your reputation is more important than the people who need your help, but I've come to teach you to be a friend of sinners. I want you to live as a citizen of the Kingdom, where no one is considered an outcast and everyone is covered and protected for all time by the eternal presence of God.

Pure

You've been told to think God is about a religion of image management, but I'm here to teach you to become absorbed in God, not our own intentions—even the purity of high intentions.

Peaceful

You've been told the way to peace is controlling your circumstances, but I'm here to tell you that you will only find peace in me. I am the Prince of Peace.

Righteous

You've been told that righteousness comes from your own efforts, but I'm here to teach you that righteousness comes from God. Because you will carry my righteousness within you, you will experience suffering and persecution, but this is a confirmation that you are in fellowship with me."

I borrow this question from Dallas Willard, who asks it in his book, *The Divine Conspiracy*: Have you ever considered that Jesus is the smartest man in the world? Would the very fact that we follow conventional wisdom instead of the commands of Jesus indicate that we don't believe he is?

chapter 4

DISHWASHER DISAGREEMENTS

My wife is a dishwasher organizer. The dishes are placed according to size, and the silverware is positioned to receive the most efficient cleaning.

One day she showed me some drop-down attachments meant to hold cups in place. I'd never noticed them before, perhaps because I take the free-form approach to dishwasher loading—that is, if it's in the machine somewhere, somehow, then surely it will get clean.

During our marriage, these conflicting styles often led to what my sweet, southern aunts would call "lively discussions." And I know my wife and I were not alone in these dishwasher dialogues; a number of years ago the *Wall Street Journal* published an article suggesting these disagreements are present in so many households that marriage counselors should start specializing in "soap and suds" therapy.

The truth is, my wife and I are polar opposites. She is structure; I am improvisation. She is detail; I am "see the forest, not just the tree." She walks into a room and immediately sees how to organize it. I look at a blank computer screen and see pirates and queens, knights and kings.

Jesus came from the Father "full of grace and truth" on his mission to bring us into the Kingdom (John 1:14 NIV). God's truth and grace work hand-in-hand, just like a couple who are polar opposites can work together when loading the dishwasher.

The danger as we follow Jesus into the Kingdom is that we can slip off the narrow path, on one side sliding into a ditch of burdensome religion—what we commonly call legalism—and on the other side sliding into a ditch where there is a presumptive disregard for the bloody cost of God's grace, something Bonhoeffer refers to as cheap grace.

Both these ditches look a little bit like following Jesus, and so we can trudge through the mud, thinking we're still hot on the heels of Jesus. But both these ditches carry us away from the intimate relationship God desires that we have with Jesus Christ. Both of these paths attempt to do the impossible: the first tries to separate grace from truth and the second tries to separate truth from grace. Either way, it only creates a monumental mess.

It's something like a dishwasher organizer crossing the line into making exacting and burdensome rules on how to load the dishes or a free-form arranger moving from creative implementation to a chaos that leaves some dishes still dirty after a wash is complete.

Bonhoeffer says either extreme will leave us perpetually immature, the one following rules instead of learning to be dependent upon Jesus and the other following impulse instead of learning to be obedient to God's Word. The idea that we can disconnect from Jesus or that some part of our life can be disconnected from Jesus is a delusion straight from the pit of hell.

Instead of seeking God, we seek our own angry solutions; it doesn't require any faith at all to wield words that blame, pointed fingers, the look that kills, a caustic tone, a slammed door, the cold shoulder, even silence and stares as punishment.

When we try to bring about righteousness by using unrighteous anger, we simply create more conflict. We develop a critical, faultfinding mentality that doesn't allow us to see the whole person, the real God-begotten person of the new creation. We're unable to see with the eyes of Jesus because we're squinting through our frozen anger.

Like Cold War conflicts once played out with surrogates in backwater ports, our arguments over the inconsequential are really substitute arguments for things of serious, even eternal, significance. It's like working together on a cure for cancer, but getting distracted by arguments over the stitching on the lab coats.

I wish my wife and I were the only ones with these arguments, but I know it's not true. James says all our fights and arguments emerge from the desires that war within us. "You want things, but you cannot have them, so you are ready to kill; you strongly desire things, but you cannot get them, so you quarrel and fight. You do not have what you want because you do not ask God for it" (James 4:2 TEV).

So you pray that your spouse will change, and you get no answer because your motives are wrong. You pray that God will help your spouse understand, and you get no answer. You pray that God will change your spouse's heart, and you get no answer. You pray God will give you grace in the matter, and you cross your fingers hoping he won't answer because what you really want is for God to make your spouse do things the way you want. In essence, you're asking God to change your spouse from a human being into the image that matches the delusion in your head.

Sometimes we skip the prayer and simply push back. We react without thinking instead of responding in love and mutual interest. We dig in to defend a position, no longer concerned about the truth, but only in winning at all costs. Soon the battle knows no bounds as it jumps the riverbank into other issues and other problems.

We no longer see a spouse or even a person; we see the opponent, and now everything the opponent says or does, even "Good morning" or the absence of "Good morning," seems related to the conflict, to winning or losing. We check the life insurance policies and then, like James and John suggested, try to call down fire from heaven to destroy our enemy (Luke 9:51-56). But the perceived enemy is someone you once swore to love and honor, in sickness and in health, until death does us part. I think about the confusion, heartache, and hard-heartedness that sets in when two people who are close stand on opposite sides of a swinging door, both pushing to open the door. It becomes exhausting, draining your energy away.

And this happens because it really is that important whether the toilet paper rolls over the top or from underneath, whether the toothpaste tube is rolled up from the bottom or squeezed by random thumbprints up and down the tube, isn't it? Just ask a precision organizer and a free-form arranger once they've transformed into a dishwasher totalitarian and a dishwasher anarchist.

And we wonder why we have trouble entering the Kingdom of Heaven. It's not that hard to see the enemy's strategy, unless you're so focused on dirty dishes that you're blind to what's going on around you. Unless you're like kids on a playground in a verbal shoving match, yelling "did to" and "did not," which might be funny except that you're adults and supposed to be beyond the mere milk that baby Christians require.

Paul says we're not even ready for solid food because we still live like the people of this world live: "When there is jealousy among you and you quarrel with one another, doesn't this prove that you belong to this world, living by its standards?" (1 Corinthians 3:3 TEV)

Bonhoeffer says only Jesus can break through our petty tyrannies, our demands to live life on our terms, and our delusions about what is important in life. To enter the Kingdom, we must come not only to the end of ourselves, but we must *alter* our lives in obedience to the Word of God, Jesus.

Only then do we enter God's grace, and Bonhoeffer says, "Such grace is costly because it calls us to follow, and it is grace because it calls us to follow Jesus Christ. It is costly because it costs a man his life, and it is grace because it gives a man the only true life. It is costly because it condemns sin, and grace because it justifies the sinner."

——— ———

Bonhoeffer taught me that the free gift of grace also carried costly responsibilities. Think of it like this: Grace is an orchestra you are invited to join. Your membership is free. It is a gift from the maestro who sees a talent in you no one else sees. But joining the orchestra will cost you everything because you have to leave other things behind as you focus on following the maestro and becoming the musician God made you to be.

> "Such grace is costly because it calls us to follow, and it is grace because it calls us to follow Jesus Christ. It is costly because it costs a man his life, and it is grace because it gives a man the only true life. It is costly because it condemns sin, and grace because it justifies the sinner."
>
> —BONHOEFFER

The maestro will demand you give up anything that distracts, anything that hinders your progress, any habit or attitude that simply isn't fitting for the grand performance to come. The maestro will not compromise in his standards of excellence; yet, every day he will be by your side, encouraging you in your development as a musician.

When some join the symphony, they refuse to give up their presumptions of what it is like to play in the orchestra. Instead of following the maestro, they follow their own formulas for how the music should be played. This is legalism and it is as much disobedience to the commands of Jesus as the rebellion we so easily cite as disobedience.

Yet, others join the orchestra and assume they don't have to work hard at becoming better musicians. They remain sloppy in their technique and they bring their bad habits into the symphony. They have no regard for the gift the maestro gave them when he invited them to join the orchestra. Some of them assume they were invited to join because of their talents and abilities, not realizing they are only there because of the word of the maestro. This is cheap grace, and it assumes we need not put serious effort into following Jesus with an abandonment that includes throwing off "everything that gets in the way" including "the sin which holds on to us so tightly" as we "run with determination the race that lies before us" (Hebrews 12:1 TEV).

But I am exhausted from the race and wonder how long I can run before I die.

chapter 5

JESUS CENTRAL

There's only one reason to get married. What is that reason?

I'll open up the phone lines and take the sixteenth caller. In the meantime, here's a long distance dedication to a young couple whose marriage got off to a rocky start.

My wife and I met at a fraternity dance. She was a hazel-eyed, fiery redhead. For those of you who stayed awake in Humanities, she looked like she'd just stepped out of a Pre-Raphaelite painting.

In today's terms, we hung out and then we hooked up. But the Bible says that God will not be mocked; your sins will find you out (Galatians 6:7).

So a few days after Thanksgiving, my (future) wife showed up, saying she was pregnant. I was skeptical and insisted on another pregnancy test. We went to the same clinic she'd been to for the previous test, and they confirmed she was pregnant, so we asked to speak to the doctor. We wanted to know if the baby would be healthy, because if it was, then we planned to keep it.

Looking back, this is an absurd question to ask, but nonetheless one that is asked all too often today. In Kingdom reality, does it really matter if the baby is healthy? God speaks you into your mother's womb, creating you the way he wants you to be.

But thirty years ago, under the guise of medical objectivity, a young doctor told us without question and with nothing more than a pelvic examination that our baby would be perfectly healthy and normal and that we should expect to be parents for a long, long time. When we told him we were keeping the baby, he said, "Having a baby is a lifetime commitment; you really need to think about what you're doing."

We sensed something wasn't right, and we left. It wasn't until later that we learned some women's health clinics exist primarily to sell abortions to women in crisis. In fact, a few years later, I interviewed Carol Everett, who once owned five abortion clinics in Dallas, and she said it was not uncommon to tell girls who were not pregnant that they were pregnant in order to sell them an abortion. Everett wrote about her experiences and how Jesus changed her life in her book, *Blood Money: Getting Rich off a Woman's Right to Choose.*

We were trying to follow a thoughtful process as we decided what to do, but the reason it is called a crisis pregnancy is because there are all sorts of emotions, pressure, guilt, and confusion that come with it. Your life is in crisis; it's common to get conflicting counsel, and it's far too easy to apply long-term solutions to short-term problems.

My wife went to an obstetrician, where she was given a basic exam. They took it for granted that she was pregnant since she told them she'd had two exams.

I was in an "oh wretched man" state that Paul speaks of—broken, and, as I told my sister, Lori, I wanted to live in the light for the rest of my life. My wife and I kept praying, asking God what to do. Adoption is a viable and God-blessed option, but neither of us felt comfortable with it. We considered that my wife could keep the baby and I could provide financial support, but I had trouble leaving her to do that alone. Besides, this was my child, too.

We talked about marriage, but, frankly, I didn't love her and I didn't think we were a good match. But even though I was coming back to the Lord, I still was worshipping an idol: the image of the nice guy. I held so rigidly to that false doctrine that it skewed my ability to submit consistently to the commands of Jesus.

When a nice guy gets a girl pregnant, he offers to marry her. She said yes. My sister, who is a nurse, cautioned us that most problems in a pregnancy show up in the first three months. If something happened to the baby, we'd still be married. She was pregnant herself at the time, and she called and said, "You know, two babies aren't any more trouble than one. I'll adopt your baby."

Her act of love and offer to bear our burden took a tremendous weight off my shoulders. I, at least, now felt like I had a choice.

My roommate at the time was bold enough to outline why my wife and I were not a good match, and, looking back, he was dead on in his analysis. But I took an arrogant view at the time and dismissed his advice because he wasn't a Christian. I've since come to understand that God can speak through anyone, and if anyone isn't available, he'll use a donkey like he did with Balaam.

Instead, we listened to a family member who was also a pastor. At first he told us to get an abortion; we dismissed that advice but missed the warning it should have given us. When we told him we were going to get married, he said, "Then you need to do it right away."

"We were thinking about a couple of months, in March or April," I said.

"No, you need to do it right away," he responded. "If not this weekend, then the next." He was giving this advice in the first week of December, and we mistook his opinion for godly direction.

Bonhoeffer expressed concern that, when faced with a critical decision, believers often argue from experience or opinion, leaving out any argument from Scripture. He says that when we give greater credence to experience or opinion, we reveal we don't "seriously read, know, and study the Scriptures."

"It is not our heart that determines our course, but God's Word," says Bonhoeffer. It is only with God's Word that we can help one another stay steadily on the narrow path, following

Jesus. It is God's Word that gives us confidence that our Father is just and loving and actively at work in our lives.

I wasn't sure why the pastor wanted us to rush into the marriage, but he was adamant: "You need to set a date in the next two weeks and tell your parents what it is and, if they can't come, tell them you're getting married anyway."

> "It is not our heart that determines our course, but God's Word."
> —BONHOEFFER

I brought up the idea of my sister adopting the baby (as I mentioned, this pastor was a family member). He rejected that option without discussion, saying it would never work because one of the grandparents would treat the baby as second class—an odd argument since the second option would be the baby living with my wife and me, where the same grandparents would be involved.

I also expressed concern that I didn't really love my wife. This is not a put-down of her but a statement of truth about an issue that should be considered before any marriage. Perhaps thinking of the concern any mother would have, the pastor told me that if my mother asked me if I loved my wife, to lie to her. She did, and I did.

And so on December 18, despite all four parents pleading with us to wait until after Christmas, we were married in a small ceremony, and, because it was all we could afford, headed off to a camping honeymoon on St. Augustine Beach in

Florida. Our wedding night turned out to be one of the coldest nights ever on the beach.

I have a picture of my wife, taken the next morning, in which she is running down the beach in an overcoat. She's turning to see me behind her, and I caught her girlish laughter by surprise. It remains my favorite picture of her. One day, when I was picking up the boys from her apartment, I noticed she had it on her wall.

After the honeymoon, we came back to the day-to-day, and I started a new job, one God provided the same week we decided to marry. It provided a significant raise that helped us as we started a new life.

One Friday, about three weeks into the marriage, the obstetrician couldn't find the baby's heartbeat, so the doctor ordered a more involved pregnancy test that would be more accurate, but it required twenty-four hours to provide results. I found out later there was another test that could actually pinpoint the length of the pregnancy, but it cost $250, so the doctor rarely recommended it.

The next morning, we received a call from the doctor personally. He told us my wife had an ectopic pregnancy and that we needed to get her to the hospital immediately. Also called a tubal pregnancy, the situation meant that the embryo was lodged in the Fallopian tube and that the baby would not survive; more critical was the damage that could be done to the mother's reproductive system, not to mention internal bleeding that could lead to her death.

Because my wife's health insurance had been through her father's work, she was dropped the day we were married, no longer being a dependent. And, of course, since she was already pregnant when I started my new job and signed us up for health insurance, this specific pregnancy was not covered. So we arrived at the hospital with no health insurance.

The doctor rushed my wife into emergency surgery and brought her out healthy but groggy. The baby was gone. I remember my struggle because the hospital room was $800 a day, and the doctor wanted my wife to stay overnight. We didn't have $1,600, and that didn't even include the doctor's bill. But a kindly nurse explained to me that the billing was based on how many nights you stayed, so the hospital bill would only be $800.

Yet, just a few days later, my wife had a positive pregnancy test, so they ordered the $250 test and sent us to the hospital for an ultrasound. The technician, perhaps not trained in speaking cautiously, pointed to a tiny spot and congratulated us on being pregnant. We were dumbfounded and explained about the ectopic pregnancy.

He brought in the radiologist, who clearly had some concerns with what he saw on the screen but was non-committal with us, saying he'd give his report to the obstetrician.

The next day my wife had a classic miscarriage, tears streaming down her face as she discharged a bloody mass. When the more accurate pregnancy test came back, we understood why the doctor had been unable to hear the baby's heartbeat: My wife was only three to four weeks pregnant. We were in our fourth week of marriage.

There's only one reason to get married. What is that reason? Because Jesus tells you to.

Regardless of the circumstances, because Jesus told you to.

What about love? God is a God of romance. Go read Song of Solomon. Look at the stories of Isaac and Rebekah, Jacob and Rachel, Boaz and Ruth.

"Whether you consider love or not, do you believe that Jesus knows who is best for you?"

> "God joins you together in marriage; it is His act, not yours. Do not confound your love for one another with God. God makes your marriage indissoluble, and protects it from every danger that may threaten it from within and without."
>
> —BONHOEFFER

Bonhoeffer writes from prison: "God joins you together in marriage; it is His act, not yours. Do not confound your love for one another with God. God makes your marriage indissoluble, and protects it from every danger that may threaten it from within and without; He wills to be the guarantor of its indissolubility. It is a blessed thing to know that no power on earth, no temptation, no human frailty can dissolve what God holds together; indeed, anyone who knows that may say confidently: What God has joined together, can no man put asunder. Free from all anxiety that is always a characteristic of love, you can now say to each other with complete and confident assurance: We can never lose each other now; by the will of God we belong to each other till death.

"From the first day of your wedding till the last the rule must be: 'Welcome one another . . . for the glory of God . . . .'That is God's word for your marriage."

——— ——

Paul says grace is a mystery, hard to explain, but perhaps we catch a glimpse of it in marriage (Ephesians 5:31-32). When you marry, you leave your old life behind and begin a new life that is other-centered. You become one with another and all of your relationships are changed because you now live within this marriage (live within grace).

It is expected that you will throw away the proverbial little black book that lists the people you have been dating or wanted to date. It is expected that you will relate to the opposite sex in a different way. You are no longer single; you are married. You belong to each other; in truth, you are joined to the other. You are one with the other.

You will also relate differently to your same-gender friends. It is expected that you won't just take off and do what you want. You are one with another. You communicate and coordinate together.

This is what our relationship with Jesus is meant to be like. We are in union with him. We are one with him in a similar way that a husband and wife are one. We cannot relate to other people in the same way we did before we became joined with Jesus.

Even the way you relate to your mother, father, sister, or brother must change, which is why Jesus says, "Those who come to me cannot be my disciples unless they love me more than they love father and mother, wife and children, brothers and sisters, and themselves as well" (Luke 14:26 TEV).

We may think we have the option, but the reality is we cannot relate to anyone as if we are separated from Jesus. We may think we can by compartmentalizing our relationships.

You can't say, "Jesus is part of my life" or "Jesus is important to my life." You now say, "Jesus defines my life."

Your ability to love others, to respond to them as eternal beings, comes from your connection with Jesus (1 John 4:11–12). When you try to relate to them in any other way, you are trying to relate as if you are no longer connected to Jesus. And when you do that, you're no longer leaning on Jesus as mediator and following him as a disciple.

When we buy into cheap grace, we assume, since we are forgiven, that we can now go back and relate to others as if we are not connected to Jesus. But we can't do that anymore than someone who's just gotten married can go back to former lovers and try to maintain a relationship with them that does not recognize the marriage. We are in union with Jesus, just as a married man and woman are in union with each other.

When we try to separate Jesus from our relationships, we deny the reality that the life of Christ is active within us. Since that life flows from Jesus through us to others, we actually have to block the flow in order to hide Jesus from our friends, family, or business associates. And this undermines the authenticity of those relationships.

Bonhoeffer adds that the world is full of little gods who want to retain their hold over you, and that is why the world is so bitterly opposed to Christ. Some of those little gods are us: We refuse to relinquish our independence from Jesus, insisting we can receive forgiveness but then return to a life of independent living.

Bonhoeffer notes that we tend to confuse our love of the world with God's love for the people who call the world home. We confuse love for the sinner with love for the sin.

chapter 6

JESUS DEFINES

Right now I'm living in the bonus room as we work through the divorce. It is like a small apartment with a bathroom of its own. The window has some decorative bars across it, and I begin to think of it as my prison window until one day a mourning dove builds her nest and nestles it inside the bars on the outer sill next to the screen. We can look directly into the frail nest, like you'd look into a terrarium. I call her Gracie because she is a blessing from God and reminds me of his provision.

"The same God who sees no sparrow fall to the ground without his knowledge and will, allows nothing to happen, except it be good and profitable for his children and the cause for which they stand," says Bonhoeffer. "We are in God's hands. Therefore, fear not."

It doesn't take long before two eggs are in the nest and my sons and I have a front row view of Gracie caring for them. She never seems to leave the nest, and we're amazed at her dedication as she sits there for days, rarely flying away and occasionally swooping down into the sprinkler.

> "The same God who sees no sparrow fall to the ground without his knowledge and will, allows nothing to happen, except it be good and profitable for his children and the cause for which they stand. We are in God's hands. Therefore, fear not."
>
> —BONHOEFFER

The mourning dove gets its name from its mournful "cooOOoo-woo-woo-woooo," a high, lonesome sound that slips into my room and lingers like a melancholy soul desperate to be found. It reminds me of a distant, desolate train whistle in the night.

It reminds me of a time when I was a young reporter working in Florida, and I wrote a story about the last days of the dusky seaside sparrow. These sparrows lived in the marshes around Merritt Island and along the St. Johns River, but sometime in the 1940s, the insecticide DDT was sprayed across the wetlands to cut down on mosquitoes. Then, when the Kennedy Space Center was built on the tip of the island, parts of their habitat were flooded, again, to control mosquitoes.

I lived on Merritt Island for a time, and from my back porch I could see the Vertical Assembly Building where they prepared the Saturn rockets to take us to the moon. One night I saw a cockroach scuttling across the kitchen floor and I stepped on it. But it wasn't a cockroach. It was a mosquito that had so engorged itself with human blood that it could no longer fly. It popped when I put my foot down, exploding gore and guts across the kitchen floor like a fast food ketchup pack slammed with a hammer.

So they kept messing with the sparrow's habitat, and by the time I did my story in 1981, there were only six dusky seaside sparrows left—all of whom were males. The last sighting of a female had been in 1975. God looks out for the sparrows, but like Eden, we spoil the environment. God ordains marriage, and because of our stubborn hearts, we put asunder his plan.

I remember ending the radio report with the mating call of the dusky seaside sparrow—a mating call with no one to answer back.

——— ——

Sometime after the divorce, I took a look at a few of the Internet dating sites. I found them intriguing, discouraging, and amusing (I only looked among the women; I've no doubt the men are just the same.)

There were women who were very specific about what they wanted in a man—eyes: steel blue (color code match #4863A0). Others seemed more flexible—height: 3'1" to 8'7."

Some posts immediately reveal a woman's temperament or relational backgrounds:

"I'm physically, spiritually, and financially fit. I expect you to be the same."

"No job. No shoes. No service. Are there any men out there who don't lie?"

"No deadbeats. No drug addicts. No projects."

"If you have a dog, know this: I was not raised in a barn. I do not live in a barn. I will not share the bed with your dog."

"I don't need anyone. I'm perfectly happy. But I would like to find someone to share my life."

I liked the directness of this one:

"When a guy needs a shirt, he drives to the mall, goes directly to the shirt counter, and buys a shirt. He does not spend five hours at the mall going in and out of every store, trying on dozens of shirts.

You need a shirt. Here is my offer.

I am looking for like-minded guys who are willing to do a quick one-stop Starbucks meet-and-greet for an instantaneous assessment. I drink a tall skinny latte with hazelnut, so meeting me will set you back $3.

You know exactly what you want in a shirt, and so do I. If I am not the right shirt, just leave the store. If I am the right shirt, tell me and I will let you know right there if we are a go. I am in favor of Match.com-inspired speed dating. I am not interested in courtship by e-mail. No guy buys a shirt by spending endless nights online e-mailing about his favorite pet.

The smart guy who understands this will not be interested in spending his nights endlessly e-mailing prospective dates, either.

Life is for living, not e-mailing, text-messaging, phone calling, and other modern-techno means of avoiding real, live, personal interaction. If this makes sense to you, please get in contact to set up the Starbucks. Thanks, and oh yes, I work in insurance sales, graduated from Purdue University, and have two wonderful and successful grown children."

I think it's funny how many 5-foot-3 women are looking for 6-foot-1 men. Okay, I get it: When you wear high heels, you're a couple of inches taller for the night and, for some women, it's important to still be shorter than your date/spouse. But 5'3" to 6'1"? Just how high are the heels you intend to wear?

But, most of all, a common thread that runs through the posts is a variation on the boulevard of broken dreams. We're all looking for love and acceptance, authenticity and trust, companionship and romance. A majority are looking for the good life; they want to travel, go out to dinner, go shopping, and prove that they really are as comfortable in that little black dress as they are in jeans.

There's nothing wrong with these things, but there's a noticeable absence of people, even on Christian sites, who want to serve Jesus. It's as if Jesus is an add-on to their lives, but that's not the way it works. Bonhoeffer teaches that Jesus must be central to our lives. He is the mediator between God and us, but he also is the mediator between us and others. When we become believers, we can never look at anyone the same. We have to look at them through the lens of Jesus and interact with them according to our relationship with Jesus.

Bonhoeffer explains: "Our hearts have room only for one all-embracing devotion, and we can only cleave to one Lord. Every competitor to that devotion must be hated. As Jesus says, there is no alternative—either we love God or we hate him."

One Christian site allows you to tell potential dates where God fits in your life. The choices: It defines who I am; it has a significant place; I'm still trying figure it out; I believe in God. I'm not knocking the site, which has a good reputation, but I looked at those choices and thought, "If you are a believer, why would you consider potential mates who don't define themselves by Jesus?"

> "Our hearts have room only for one all-embracing devotion, and we can only cleave to one Lord. Every competitor to that devotion must be hated. As Jesus says, there is no alternative—either we love God or we hate him."
>
> —BONHOEFFER

But Bonhoeffer suggests such choices reflect the modern church. We've taught people it's okay to let Jesus have a significant place in their lives, a moderate place in their lives, or a compartmentalized place in their lives. I'm not talking about nonbelievers who are seeking, and we know discipleship involves growth, so people need to grow into "Jesus defines my life."

But the growth isn't happening among so many followers of Christ. Why, instead of the abundant life, do so many of us end up living lives of *quiet desperation*? We go to church, we read the Bible, we pray, we try to be good people and to serve other people. Yet, for many of us, Jesus isn't central to our increasingly complex lives, where we're over-stretched and now seem to be facing a tsunami of uncertainty in many areas that for so long have seemed relatively secure, such as our finances, our jobs, our homes—even our fundamental safety.

The core of Bonhoeffer's theology is that Jesus must be central to our lives and central to the church. Jesus was never meant to be an important part of our lives; he *is* our life (Colossians 3:4). If you try to find your life apart from Jesus, you will lose it; but if you lose your life in Jesus, then you will live an extraordinary life energized by the life of Christ within you.

Bonhoeffer says we've been lulled into believing there are two tiers to discipleship—sort of like cable plans, with basic channels and a premium package for the more pious. We delude ourselves, thinking there are but a few among us— monks, missionaries, and ministers—who are called to be more saintly, while the rest of us must settle comfortably into a mediocre, part-time discipleship.

Jesus, on the other hand, will not tolerate wishy-washy disciples. Clearly, what we call radical obedience here on earth is *the obedience expected in the Kingdom of Heaven*. In other words, our lukewarm discipleship is actually radical *dis*obedience.

Jesus has his eye on the endgame, and so Bonhoeffer says Christ intends to breakthrough every program, every ideal, and every form of legalism that keeps us from following him in total abandonment. "No other significance is possible, since Jesus is the only significance. Beside Jesus nothing has any significance. He alone matters," Bonhoeffer says.

When my wife and I were married, we agreed to put Jesus at the center of our marriage. In this day and age, it is the only way any marriage can survive. We gave our testimony about how God was working in our lives and that Jesus was at the center of our marriage.

And we meant every word we said, and God *was* working significantly in our lives and in our marriage. But you know what I think happened? Jesus was *near* the center of our marriage, just slightly off axis so that the rotation had a wobble to it that was imperceptible in the early years—but, like a top that's slowing down, each year the wobble became more pronounced until eventually we were swinging out of control.

From a Nazi concentration camp, Bonheoffer wrote a wedding sermon for two friends, saying, "God gives you Christ as the foundation of your marriage. 'Welcome one another, therefore, as Christ has welcomed you, for the glory of God' (Romans 15:7). In a word, live together in the forgiveness of your sins, for without it no human fellowship, least of all a marriage, can survive. Don't insist on your rights, don't blame each other, don't judge or condemn each other, don't find fault with each other, but accept each other as you are, and forgive each other every day from the bottom of your hearts."

Bonhoeffer was engaged while in prison and he wrote passionate, romantic letters to his fiancé that also revealed Jesus was at the center of their relationship. He was uncertain when he would be released, but he was certain that God was in control.

Although my wife and I both contributed to our marriage being off-center, God revealed one area of disobedience that I resisted. Regardless of the circumstances of our marriage or how I felt at the beginning, my wife was now my wife, and I needed to abandon any loyalty to another, including any fantasies of the perfect mate or the perfect marriage.

This was a two-by-four in my eye that hindered me from seeing things clearly and undermined any efforts by me to help my wife with the splinter in her own eye.

Looking back, it seems odd, but I gave this fantasy such significance that I didn't think I could live without it. Our fantasies—Bonhoeffer might call them delusions—may be defense mechanisms against a harsh reality, but Jesus wants us to bring them into his light. He will only pour his grace into the "now" of our lives, not into any idolatrous inventions.

Following Jesus means we must stay in the present and cooperate with him as he works through our circumstances, no matter how difficult they seem. This is essential to our ability to mature into the fullness of Christ. By giving our lives over to delusions, we avoid the very issues and circumstances God wants to use to bring us to spiritual maturity.

One day I sat on my bed and told God, "I can't break this stronghold. I need you to do it. I confess I have often been more loyal to my fantasy than to my own wife. I am desperate, and I need you to uproot and destroy this stronghold."

Perhaps I fell asleep, but I don't think I did. I heard a noise and, as it got louder, it sounded like a train clanging down the tracks. The sound of the train got closer, and then I started to think it might be a tornado. I'd heard a similar sound when a twister ran through Topeka, Kansas, when I was a small boy.

I looked out the window, and it was a bright, sunny day. It seemed as if the noise swept into my room, streaked into my right ear and out the left. As it exited, there was a loud pop. I lay there for a moment and realized something had changed. I felt a sense of release. I was certain that God had uprooted the stronghold and, as each day passed, I found it to be true.

chapter 7

CONCRETE FAITH

If I'd known it would be our last lunch with Kathryn, I would have savored every moment. As it was, it took forever to get our meals and refills, and I was impatient, even more so when my wife said she didn't feel well and wanted to go. Then it took longer to get the check.

We were visiting my parents for the weekend, and by the time we got back to their house, my wife was in labor. Not Braxton Hicks kicks, but serious, "get to the hospital now" labor.

We were two and a half hours from home, and, knowing how important our regular obstetrician was to my wife, I wanted to make a mad dash to him. But the doctor said that from the facts we gave him, he didn't think we could make it: "Get her to a hospital right away."

By the time we checked in with the nurses, my wife's cervix was dilated six centimeters. They were friendly and deliberate but in no particular hurry until I mentioned she was only twenty-three weeks pregnant. There was a pause, where both nurses looked at each other through widening eyes, and then a lot of motion all at once: sweeping my wife into a birthing room, informing the doctor on call, wires and monitors and IVs appearing from nowhere.

What everybody knew but wasn't saying is that the best chance for a premature baby to survive outside the womb is that she be at least twenty-four weeks *in utero*. Kathryn was one crucial week short, but she wasn't going to wait.

The doctor—considered one of the best by the nurses—showed up as my wife and I were talking about ways to save the baby. Should she have a C-section? What could we do to help Kathryn survive? The doctor said, "Look, you can do the heroic thing here, but I don't think the baby has a chance to survive an operation. My concern right now is for the mother—not only making sure she's healthy, but that we take every care to ensure she can have other children."

This was the moment when I stopped following formulas of faith and began following Jesus in faith. The problem with our religious systems, our methods and formulas, is that no matter how well intentioned, they tend to lead us away from Jesus. Rather than asking him what we should do in a given situation, we begin to assume we know what Jesus would have us do.

This takes the immediacy out of our relationship with Jesus. Instead of asking him, "What would you have me do now?" we make choices based on our formulas and pre-conceived notions of what a Christian should do.

In that moment of decision, we asked Jesus what we should do, and we sensed he was telling us to go with a natural birth. We wouldn't do anything to harm Kathryn, and she truly would be in God's hands as she came through the birth canal.

——— ——

Bonhoeffer says Jesus calls us to a concrete faith. We can't just have faith in general; we must take specific steps of faith—visible, concrete steps. And the steps can't just be anything; they must be the steps Jesus tells us to take. We can take great risks, thinking they will please Jesus, but unless Jesus initiates them, they are faithless steps.

What Jesus does, says Bonhoeffer, is continually push us into new situations that will require us to trust him. It "is the impossible situation in which everything is staked solely on the word of Jesus," says Bonhoeffer.

> What Jesus does, says Bonhoeffer, is continually push us into new situations that will require us to trust him. It "is the impossible situation in which everything is staked solely on the word of Jesus."

When Jesus called Peter to step out of the boat and walk to him across the water, the disciple didn't just jump out of the boat and yell, "Catch me, Lord, I'm coming!" He asked Jesus to call him, and Peter only stepped onto the water after Jesus told him to come on. It was a call to give up voluntarily the security of the boat for the insecurity of walking on rough water (Matthew 14:22-31).

As Peter put his foot down on the water, he was totally dependent upon Jesus. He was taking an irrevocable step, because either Jesus would help him walk on water or Peter would sink beneath the waves.

Peter took the first step and, in that moment, he believed. His faith increased because he saw that Jesus was coming through. Then, he took another step, and his faith increased even more because he saw the consistency of Jesus. Obedience doesn't merely reflect faith; obedience leads to faith.

Too often we approach problems with our eyes limited to the things below, again discounting the truth that reality encompasses the unseen, the Kingdom, and our relationship with Jesus. And, Bonhoeffer argues, this means we eliminate faith from the situation.

You may think this an odd example, but I think that, because it is extreme, it gives clarity to Bonhoeffer's point. He says, "Lust is impure because it is unbelief, and therefore it is to be shunned." In other words, it requires faith to be faithful and faith to remain pure.

But the way we tend to approach this is through behavior management. For instance, I can block pornographic websites from my computer, but that doesn't block the lust in my heart. Now, there's nothing wrong with behavior management if it is used to help us settle into our relationship with Jesus and as long as we understand it will never help us earn our way into the Kingdom.

It is a problem if behavior management begins to replace our relationship with Jesus. That is, I fight temptation by reminding myself it is wrong by memorizing Scripture, by willing myself not to sin.

But it really is a faith issue. When you are tempted, you have a choice: You either believe fulfilling your lust is best for you or you believe that the reason Jesus condemns lust is because he knows it will keep you from becoming all that you can be. Will you put your faith in Jesus or your impulses?

This eliminates all our arguments and rationalizations to sin. Do we believe Jesus or not? Will we let Jesus have the final word on our circumstances or not? This makes your relationship with Jesus very personal; you can no longer maintain an abstract view of Jesus because you clearly see the relationship. The Incarnation is personal, and that makes our sins very personal within our relationship with Jesus.

Will I take a concrete step of faith and not give in to temptation? Will I instead trust that Jesus knows what he is talking about, knows I am not missing out on something, knows this will only hurt me, knows God will never tempt me beyond my ability to handle it, knows God will give me a way out?

Do I believe God will supply my needs through the spouse he has planned for me or has already given me? Do I believe God will give me grace in a dysfunctional circumstance?

I can block pornography, but the real issue is letting Jesus transform my heart. That transformation, Bonhoeffer says, then "liberates marriage from selfish, evil desire, and consecrates it to the service of love, which is possible only in a life of discipleship."

And since overcoming temptation is a faith issue, every step we take away from our sin gives us greater strength to say no to our sin—in the same way that every concrete step of faith we take increases our faith in Jesus.

——— ——

Kathryn's heartbeat was strong as she entered the birth canal. We heard it as a rhythmic beep coming from a monitor attached to my wife's belly. We prayed for Kathryn and talked to her, letting her know Mommy and Daddy were waiting for her. I looked at my wife and said, "What a miracle of God this will be when Kathryn survives at twenty-three weeks."

But, suddenly, her heartbeat slowed. Only slightly, but you could tell the rhythm was different. And then it slowed again, more noticeably. We encouraged Kathryn again: "We can't wait to see you." But the fetal monitor became a countdown to Kathryn's death. You could hear her heart getting weaker and weaker as its rhythm became slower and slower.

I looked at one of the nurses and said, "Can you turn that off?" She did, and my wife, in labor for her dead daughter, began to cry.

We had Kathryn cremated because that's all we could afford. It was another faith decision, because we knew some theologians considered it wrong, while others considered it acceptable. We prayed about it and studied the Bible and believed Jesus was giving us the freedom to do it.

What followed was a one-car, two-person funeral procession through the sleepy Florida towns that line U.S. 441 from Orlando to Gainesville, where we lived. With headlights on, my wife and I drove in meditative silence, carrying Kathryn's remains.

At Kathryn's funeral, I shared this: "God says 'I have plans for you. Plans to prosper you and not to hurt you.' That is the truth, and that is what we have to cling to no matter what our circumstances seem to indicate. For instance, I wondered why this happened out-of-town when we had been so careful to find a very special doctor here in town, one who has been caring for my wife for six years. But I sensed God telling me, 'Don't place your faith in doctors, place your faith in me.'"

We prayed that Kathryn would live. Does that mean God didn't answer our prayers? I think he did answer by doing what was best, but we're so blind, we're so limited in our perspective, that we often don't know what's best for us, and we ask for things that we'd never ask for if we saw God's big picture.

It's not uncommon for us to say, "It's good to trust in God, but . . . " My gentle response to that is, "It's good to trust in God . . . period." If God is not our God in time of trouble, then he is not God at all. He is nothing more than a set of laws or a written code. Yet so many of us, my wife and I included, throw our beliefs overboard just when we need them most.

Who are we trusting in, then: God or a written code? Trust means you have faith, and faith is being sure of what you hope for and certain of what you do not see. Is it enough to know that right now we see through the glass darkly if we also know the time will come when we will see reality whole and face-to-face? At present, all we know is a little fraction of the truth, but the time will come when we shall know it as fully as God has known us.

We serve a God of hope, and our hope is an anchor for our souls. And I believe that is why God tells us that we can count it all joy when we go through trials and tribulations. That doesn't mean we should be happy when we suffer a loss such as this. But it does mean that we can have confidence that a just and loving and merciful Father is working all this out for the good of his perfect will. And we can rejoice, because God can use moments like these to reveal to us where we have anchored our hope. Have we anchored it on a lie, or have we anchored it on nothing less than Jesus' blood and righteousness?

It wasn't uncommon for me to find my wife reading God's Word to our baby girl. Kathryn may not have understood the depth of the gospel, but what she did understand—the gospel according to Kathryn, if you will—is that even the darkness is light to him. Maybe none of us would struggle so much if we understood it that simply.

chapter 8

OBEDIENCE

After I graduated from college but before my wife and I were married, I was drifting in double-mindedness. Living as I pleased, I also sensed the grip of God on my heart, calling me back to an intimate relationship with Jesus. I had a stack of *Playboy* magazines and my Bible sitting side-by-side on a shelf. Seeking God while still seeking sin, I insisted that God give me insight into my future and only then would I give up the things I knew he wanted me to.

I remember having a dream during that time. I was sitting in the front, passenger side of a car, and my sister and cousin were both in the backseat. They were (and are) very committed followers of Jesus. The driver's seat was empty. You know how there are things in dreams that you just know even though you don't see it or even though nobody says it? I knew that we were waiting for Jesus to climb into the driver's seat.

I wondered why we were still waiting. What was keeping him? And my sister said, "It's because you'll miss your friends, right?" Just then, my eyes popped open, and I was awake.

"Tell me what you want me to do, Lord," I said. "Just tell me what you want me to do."

A few days later, my pastor from high school was in town leading a revival. While he was preaching, I suddenly got the impression he was speaking directly to me. Not the pastor speaking, but God speaking to me through him. Perhaps you've had that experience. It's as if the preacher's been reading your mail or as if he's actually gotten into your head.

You look around to see if everyone is staring at you, but they seem to be in another dimension, attentively listening to the sermon. You look back at the pastor, and he's not even looking at you. But his words are like a cruise missile arching through the congregation, turning slightly to avoid a tall man, and heading at supersonic speed directly into your soul.

The preacher said, "This is what God is saying to you. Don't ask me what I want you to do until you are doing the things you already know you should do."

In other words, you know to get rid of the sin in your life; you know to study the Bible; you know to pray and to be in fellowship. Do those things, show your obedience in those things, and then God will tell you what is next.

Bonhoeffer says most of the time when we're struggling with faith we're actually struggling with obedience to Jesus. He requires that we be single-minded and immediate in our obedience to his commands. Through our obedience, God puts us into a place where we can deepen our faith by taking the next step of faith.

——— ———

If you want to start a heated debate among a group of Christians, just bring up Paul's admonition that wives should submit to their husbands. But that debate is a distraction from the bigger issue: All Christians must submit to Jesus.

Bonhoeffer has convinced me that the number one reason so many of us are stuck in spiritual immaturity is that we *commit* to Christ rather than *submit* to Christ.

The difference is this: We may commit to bringing dinner rolls to the church social and have the best of intentions to provide them, even getting off work early in order to serve our locally famous, family-recipe yeast delicacy. But no one expects you to quit your job and spend all your savings in order to provide the rolls, let alone center your whole life on the rolls. In fact, people would think you were crazy.

> Bonhoeffer has convinced me that the number one reason so many of us are stuck in spiritual immaturity is that we *commit* to Christ rather than *submit* to Christ.

Have we reduced following Jesus to a similar commitment? If we're barely willing to adjust our schedules to serve Jesus, is there any hope we'll adjust our whole lives?

Commitment still leaves us in control, deciding, according to our own agendas, when or where we'll serve Jesus. Submission means we yield to the will of Christ and do what he tells us to do day in and day out, *altering* our lives in obedience to him and his Word.

Jesus makes it very plain that it is an either/or decision. We cannot live for Christ and live for ourselves. As Paul explains, "It is no longer I who live, but it is Christ who lives in me. This life that I live now, I live by faith in the Son of God, who loved me and gave his life for me" (Galatians 2:20 TEV).

Bonhoeffer adds, "The life of discipleship can only be maintained so long as nothing is allowed to come between Christ and ourselves—neither the law, nor personal piety, nor even the world." We cannot submit to Christ and still arrange things to suit ourselves; we cannot treat discipleship like a career we map out for ourselves, saying, "I'll do this for Jesus after I get the kids through school and build my retirement fund."

> "The life of discipleship can only be maintained so long as nothing is allowed to come between Christ and ourselves— neither the law, nor personal piety, nor even the world."
>
> —BONHOEFFER

Paul suggests our submission to Christ should look like an Olympic athlete training for the games, sacrificing many things in order to focus on the one. We must see the Kingdom of Heaven like the man who finds hidden treasure in a field. He re-sorts all of his priorities because nothing is as important as buying the field. We must become like the shopkeeper who finds a rare pearl and realizes everything else he has pales in comparison, so he never looks back to the things that were once important (Matthew 13:44-50).

Where we have been loyal to many things, we must now be loyal to one thing: the person, Jesus Christ.

When I lived in Florida, at least once a year an alligator would crawl out of the canals that run through neighborhoods near a river or the ocean. You'd hear about the heroic family dog, often a golden retriever, rushing to attack in order to give mom the chance to get the kids into the house.

The sound bites are always similar. "Goldie saved our lives. She started barking and when I looked out the window, I saw her standing between the alligator and my children. So I ran to get the kids inside the house, but when I turned to call Goldie, she wasn't there. Only the tennis ball they were playing with was left. We haven't seen her since."

Dogs are known for their loyalty, and among dogs, golden retrievers are considered the most loyal. Call me a golden retrieverwhich may be why I was stunned the day a moving van backed up to the house and strangers began to pack up things that for almost twenty-five years had been ours, but now were divided between hers and mine.

Despite asking for an extra six months in the house (with me living in a separate apartment-like bonus room), my wife, without telling me, had decided to take the boys and leave house. Ironically, the boys were scheduled to stay with me that night and it left us with no kitchenware to cook with and no beds for the boys to sleep in. It was an eye-opening welcome to our new life.

My wife is a good mother, and so I chose to believe that she was acting out of fear instead of faith. Every one of us faces such a choice, often on a daily basis. Will we respond in fear or will we respond in faith? In fact, let me balance this by saying we act out of fear when we submit to anything other than the will of Christ, and, therefore, my clinging to the image of a nice guy, trying to act like a good Christian would act, was no less faithless. We are called to become what Jesus wants us to become; he is busy transforming us into his image, not the image of a Christian that we cling to in our heads. We cannot mature into the real image of Christ until we toss away the false image. And if we do not toss it away, then Jesus, in loving ruthlessness, will expose the false image and destroy it because his eye is on the endgame and he knows what is at stake as we follow him into the Kingdom of Heaven.

My friend, Steve Pettit, says that whenever we are faced with conflicting loyalties Jesus should always get the highest priority. This echoes Bonhoeffer, who says Jesus will not share this top spot with anyone or anything else. In truth, we can measure our obedient trust in Jesus by looking at who gets our highest loyalty in any given situation.

Jesus is the reality, the practical, the relevant: When we are engaged in Kingdom living, then we will see all other things through him and that nothing apart from him is either relevant or practical. This viewpoint should change everything about the way we live. Bonhoeffer says only the things given to us from Jesus are God-given and part of Kingdom-reality. Whatever we received apart from Jesus is not from God.

Jesus says our relationship with him will even affect the way we relate to our families. Apart from Jesus, our relationships become impractical, impossible–and, ultimately, dysfunctional. This doesn't mean people can't have loving, supportive families apart from Jesus, and it is noteworthy that in this day and age there are some couples who do not relate to Jesus yet remain married for decades.

But the huge divorce rate is a reflection of the truth that many couples, including those who are church-going, try to live in the impractical, even impossible situation, where Jesus does not have the highest loyalty in their marriage. This only opens the door to conflicting loyalties and that leads, inevitably, to arguments, small and large, as each individual gives his and her highest loyalty to things other than Jesus. Jesus says that what we treasure will reveal the loyalty of our heartswhich is why we must treasure Jesus above all other things (Matthew 6:21).

God's design is for Christ to be the treasured center of all our relationships; this is the Creator's design for how we should live together. With Kingdom eyes, your spouse becomes an eternal being you must love and respect. You see the truth that your decisions are related to eternity: Will you learn to love your spouse into the Kingdom of God? Will you see the long-term consequences of your relationship? Will you submit your decisions, your behavior, your attitudes, your reactions, your words, and your life to Jesus? Will you see Jesus working in your circumstances? Will you walk in faith, regardless of the fearful or threatening situation you face? Will you filter everything through Jesus or will you filter them through delusions that falsely define everything in your situation as "me against you," one winner and one loser?

It was an ultra-sound that pushed me toward a proper view of obedience, although, typical for me, it came in fits and starts. Within the fluid images of a black and white monitor, we could see Jeremy's heart beating like the rhythm of the saints. We watched in joy, oblivious to our slide toward one of those significant seconds that delineates a moment before and a moment after.

His heartbeat is unmistakable. It's a pulsating light within a swirl of grey and black, a sweet beat that taps out a Morse code for life—a human being in his first crude communication: "Who-ville calling: We are here, we are here!"

The Horton in you hears the Who, and your heart hops into sync with the happy beat. It's a rhythm of joy and a rhythm of anticipation. The dance is on, and the song so saturates your soul that you can't help but swing and sway as the spirit-singer sings, "Rejoice Who-ville! We can hear, we can hear!"

There's a subtle backbeat of sobering stewardship, tapping out the natural fears and doubts that accompany this most basic human dance—the parent-to-child advance of the whole, DNA blood-to-blood race that's accomplished one precarious relationship at a time.

But this rhythm's got the blues, only you haven't noticed yet. Right now it sounds more like the Four Tops than Muddy Waters, and you're pulled into a trance, watching watery Rorschach-like images moving fluidly on the screen.

It isn't until later—slight minutes removed from the dance of joy—that the doctor quietly, deliberately says he sees something in the shifting images. You smile. You concentrate on keeping the smile sturdy even as the landscape behind it begins to crumble. You realize you're standing in a significant second, and already there's a time before and a time beyond, and you're free-falling into a future that isn't part of your calendar.

The doctor says he sees something. He calls it a cystic hygromas, and it appears to be on a ventricle in the baby's heart—the very center of the sweet beat.

He says it could be nothing, and you think that's the first sign it is something. Why talk about nothing? He says these things appear all the time at this stage of fetal development, and they often disappear. But he also warns that if it doesn't disappear, it signals a problem pregnancy—perhaps Downs Syndrome, perhaps a baby who will not survive.

You hear what the doctor says, yet you're left stuck in the moment, even as the seconds dash away.

"Whoville, we are here and we are sick."

chapter 9

LOYALTY

We've been sent to a genetic specialist. Yes, he says, the diagnosis is accurate.

And "no," he continues, "there's not really anything we can do to save this child."

Then he adds: "A Trisomy 18 baby is so universally accepted within the medical community as non-viable that we can deliver it anytime you want."

I say, "Wait a minute. You don't deliver a baby who's only been in the womb sixteen weeks."

He says he'll give my wife a pill, and she'll miscarry within a day or two.

We tell him that's not our intention. We're Christians. We believe the baby, as a creation of God, deserves dignified treatment. We're going to carry it—him . . . Jeremy—all the way to term, if possible.

He says that's fine, and that he's here to help us "rational-ize" whatever we need to get us through this crisis, working within our particular belief parameters. I sense the doctor is truly trying to be helpful within the limitations of his "belief parameters." We're in the office of a scientist, speaking the truth as he sees it within this world's perspective.

But my wife and I have learned that forty weeks or less in utero may be the breadth of one lifetime. However short, it's always a life sent from the Creator and worthy of celebrating.

The doctor is speaking again. He says we're the most mature couple he's ever met. We know it's not maturity but rather the Holy Spirit, and tomorrow we may fall apart. The doctor offers that he's a nihilist—don't worry, I had to look that up, too. It means he believes everything is random, all life is chance, and that we just got a bad roll of the dice with Jeremy.

But Scripture teaches that nothing is random. "The die is cast, but its every direction is from the Lord." Jeremy and his quirky DNA and his Trisomy 18—none of that was an accident if we believe what we say we believe.

We named him after the prophet Jeremiah, to whom God said, "Before I formed you in the womb, I knew you." Who says a life of forty weeks is any less valuable than one of eighty years?

For some reason, our Sovereign has strangely drawn my wife and me into a double decade of raising a standard for life—one lost child at a time.

F. Scott Fitzgerald once wrote, "Show me a hero, and I'll write you a tragedy." I submit to you a modern hero—a

Pre-Raphaelite redhead, who, in a treacherous age of choice, embraced one more pregnancy, sustaining life for one of God's more fragile creations when the wise of this world suggested such a thing was foolish.

But, then, God's wisdom confounds the wise of this world, and young Jeremy is no less his wisdom than our beautiful, living son.

——— ——

One week during the divorce, I took my oldest son to Gatlinburg for a special rafting trip, sensitive to the fact that soon he would no longer be living with me. He was only thirteen, but I got a glimpse of the man he will become when another raft flipped near us, and my son was able to lean out of our raft and catch one of the people who'd been thrown into the water. It reminded me of the time when he was about seven and he sprang across the room, grabbing his toddler brother who was about to stick his finger into an electrical socket that had somehow lost its safety plug.

While my oldest son and I were on our trip, my youngest son was having what he continues to describe as one of his favorite weeks because he got to live up in my "apartment" while I was gone. He called me one morning incredibly excited because Gracie's eggs had hatched, and there were two baby birds in the nest.

Gracie faithfully watched over them until, one day, they took a plunge out of the nest, sort of falling with style like Buzz Lightyear. They bounced on the ground and sat there helpless for a bit, then flew a short distance, then flew away. Ah, they grow up so fast.

The nest sat empty for a while but then, one day, Gracie showed up again and laid two more eggs. I looked at her through the glass and said, "Gracie, don't you know how to say 'no?'" Again Gracie stayed in the nest faithfully, night and day.

Since Gracie was back, I decided to do some research on mourning doves, and I discovered they are faithfully attached to their mates. I wasn't seeing one bird sitting on the nest twenty-four hours a day; I was seeing two. Dad would sit on the nest from morning through the afternoon; Mom's shift was the afternoon through the night. They are devoted parents, rarely leaving the nest and willing to put themselves at risk to save their hatchlings from a predator.

> Bonhoeffer notes that the birds and the lilies "glorify their Creator, not by their industry, toil or care, but by a daily unquestioning acceptance of his gifts."

Dad picks out several nest sites; Mom chooses which one they will build in. Dad will then fly around bringing back twigs, needles, and grass to build the nest, and then he'll stand on mom's back, handing her the material, while she constructs the nest.

Bonhoeffer notes that the birds and the lilies "glorify their Creator, not by their industry, toil or care, but by a daily unquestioning acceptance of his gifts." A characteristic of fallen thinking is that there is a "cause and effect between work and sustenance, but Jesus explodes that illusion. According to him, bread is not to be valued as the reward for work; he speaks instead of the carefree simplicity of the man who walks with him and accepts everything as it comes from God."

To echo Martin Luther, "Who put the food that the birds will find where they could find it?" Understanding this drives us deeper into Kingdom thinking. Jesus topples the mythology that what you do is a measure of what you are worth, which is just another variation on faithlessly thinking or behaving as if you can earn your way into God's good graces. We cheapen grace when we say the work of Jesus provides for our salvation but doesn't have anything to do with our survival or sustenance here on earth.

——— ——

Jeremy became my son the morning I made arrangements for his funeral. I guess the more accurate statement is this: I became Jeremy's father that morning. He was already my son by then; of that, there was no doubt.

But when I signed the legal document for the handling of Jeremy's remains, I felt a weight move onto my shoulders. Maybe the weight was already there, I don't know—but in that moment I recognized the enormity of . . . of my responsibility for being the boy's father, for making monumental decisions on his behalf. The cellophane wrap was off the package, and I owned my daddy duties for a son I hardly knew. This son, I'm told, is dying.

I called in late to work so I could get the funeral stuff out of the way and prepare for the worst but hope for the best. The best? Well, he's not dead yet, and maybe—yes, God, please—maybe he won't die at all. I mean maybe he won't die now; we all die sometime, but maybe he'll live a few more years, maybe he'll live a lifetime.

The thing is, it seemed like such an ordinary day. There I was with a list of errands—return the movies, stop by the bank, pick up some milk, make arrangements for the boy's funeral. Just another day, right? Could I will it so?

Pulling into the parking lot at the funeral home, I noticed the dogwoods. They were white with blossoms, and after getting out of the car I stood there for a long moment watching the trees sway slowly in a breeze that smelled spring-clean.

I closed my eyes and listened to the breeze shush the baby buds like a nursemaid's tender whisper: "Sh-sh-sh. Don't worry, you're right on time; yes, sweet beauty, you were dead in winter, but now you've been raised in the newness of life."

I let out a long, deep sigh. It seemed involuntary, and with it I became aware of soreness in my neck. My eyes still closed, I tilted my head side-to-side. I wanted to slip into sleep.

My focus moved slowly—the light breeze, the sh-sh-shush of playful branches, the resurrection smell of spring. From somewhere there is laughter; nearby, there is traffic—I lean toward illusive warmth and tighten my eyes, willing that when I open them, I'll be standing on the plaza enjoying a beautiful spring day in college. Pretty girls in flip-flops are walking by, laughing, talking about graduation—and real life—just a few weeks away.

I open my eyes, but I'm still in the funeral home parking lot. I'm still staring at the dogwoods. The day seems darker, though—at least darker than it should this early in the day. From somewhere comes more laughter, and I look through the dancing dogwood branches, and there I catch a clash of images—a centuries old cemetery with weatherworn head-stones that create a crooked path up a shallow slope to a historic church.

And there, beyond the graves, is the source of the laughter: little boys and girls following their moms. Their giggles run circles around the I-wish-I-had-your-energy moms, who are leading them toward a caravan of mini-vans.

You need to change. This thought floats across my head.

"You need to become like these little children. Do you see that their joy comes from living in the moment? You can have that joy when you stop thinking you must be in control and instead trust that I Am in control."

I say out loud, "It seems darker to me than it should for this time of day, God. What's that all about?"

And then speaking soft and low, I say, "I hear you, God, but I'm . . . numb . . . for now. You're in charge; you've got control; and we both know there isn't a bloody thing I can do. I've got it—you're God and I am not."

"But that doesn't mean I have to agree with this; or that I have to feel good about it." And I think, but don't say, "Sir, yes, sir."

Once again, I let out a loud, long sigh, and become aware of just how very tired I am. I nod to the dogwoods and head across the parking lot into the funeral parlor.

Inside, well, yes, it is deathly quiet, except for the unceasing beat of a grandfather clock measuring the ticky-tock of each second. Being an old grandfather, it should be mindful of the finality of each beat, experienced enough to know that lives begin and end with each second. But the dotty old man snaps out a cadence that suggests everything is on time and under control, ever steady, moving on and keeping on. He is locked into the cadence of time, unable to stop—for even a second—to reflect upon the carnage of the time he measures. That's okay, I do enough reflecting for the both of us.

The funeral director has a box of tissues on his desk, a necessary tool of his trade.

He pulls a document from a desk drawer and asks, "Name of the deceased?"

"Well, he's not dead yet."

"I'm so sorry. I just need to get his name for the documents."

"I understand. His name is Jeremy. Jeremy Clark Walker."

"You're relationship to Jeremy?"

"I'm his father." His daddy, I think, as the funeral director works down the form.

I close my eyes, and I'm pedaling my bike as fast as I can. My own daddy runs beside me. I'm on my brand-new, red Coast-to-Coast bicycle, complete with thick, white-wall tires, matching white ribbons snapping from the wide handlebars, and on the back is a flat bumper for toting my treasures. I've already tried to strap the family dog to the bumper-seat, but it didn't quite work out as I had planned.

The bike is too big for my legs, so I push the pedals with the tips of my toes. We're racing for home after my challenge: "Dad, I bet I can beat you there!"

His military dog-tags give a muffled jingle under his flight suit; he's running in his flight boots. He pushes his arms in poetic precision, his knees arching high, and he tosses me a smile as he stays right by my side, steady and unwavering. He must be superhuman, I think, because he's keeping up with a bicycle, the fastest bike I've ever known. And I'm going as fast as I can. I try, but I can't go any faster. My dad is strong; my dad is undefeatable.

But I'm not that strong; I'm not a warrior-hero. The present pushes into the past and, in my mind, I turn toward Colonel Walker and say what I'd say if my Dad were still alive: "I'm not sure I can do this. I'm not that strong." Only it's me—I mean, the adult me—on the bike. It's me saying I can't do this to my Dad.

I say, "I don't think I can carry this burden."

He says, "You're stronger than you think."

But then, there it is in my hand—the form—giving permission to the funeral parlor to handle the remains of my son, Jeremy. I pretend to be reading the document thoroughly, but my mind is marching through thoughts of the things you might sign on behalf of a child: a nursery school registration, a permission slip to go to camp, a financial aid form for college, a document for disposing of your son's remains.

I unconsciously give another heavy sigh, then I reinforce my practiced poker face. It's just another day; it's just another item on my to-do list. I sign the document and look, for just a grampa-clock second, at the first official printing of Jeremy's name.

I shake hands with the funeral director, but I'm not really paying much attention to the good-bye. I'm walking the depths of my imagination, desperately trying to find a way out of the harsh, hot light of reality.

I'm a king and Jeremy is my heir. I'm Théoden, King of Rohan, and I'm speaking to Aragorn, who is the prophetic king returning to defeat the evil lord of the rings. I look through eyes that have carried a burden far too long, but I know the end is still a long, long time away.

I tell Aragorn, "A father shouldn't have to bury his children." And I look away, but when I look back, Aragorn is no longer there. I'm looking into the eyes of Jesus—my king, Jesus.

Tears well in my eyes, and I say, "A father shouldn't have to bury his children. I don't think I can do this; I'm not that strong."

Jesus says, "I am strong, and therefore, you are strong. Let me be your strength."

"Please, you have the power to grant my request," I say. "Take this thing away; take this pain away; don't make me face this." Then, in a tone so desperate that it surprises me and leaves me feeling uncomfortable: "Please!"

My lips tremble and I fight against a deep, long frown that is pushing with surprising strength in an effort to re-cast my face—my practiced poker face. I look down, take in a deep breath, and gather myself. I know if I let go, then I'll slip into uncontrolled tears—chaotic, uncontained, mob rule.

In a hollow, hoarse whisper, I say, "Do what you have to do; it's not up to me." And I look into the eyes of my Jesus.

I'm surprised by his response: "Even though you are an imperfect father, you still know how to give good gifts to your children. Don't you think the Father in heaven knows what to do as well?"

I find myself standing next to my car. My head feels like I've just been jerked awake from a deep sleep; I'm disoriented. Sluggishly, my gaze returns to the dogwoods, and the thought is already in my head that they're a reminder of God's faithfulness.

There in my memory is a vision of a vision: God using a vision of a tree in the spring to teach the ancient prophet Jeremiah that the seasons are God's monument to infinite faithfulness, "Year in and year out, you trust the seasons to return. Now, Jeremiah, tell my people to trust that I am just as faithful."

In the vision, God shows Jeremiah a branch from the almond, the first tree in ancient Israel to bloom in spring. It's known as the "watch tree," and God, with a twinkle in his eye, tosses the weeping prophet a humorous play on words.

God, the Creator: Jeremiah, what do you see?

Jeremiah, a created one: I see a branch from the 'watch' tree.

God, our Creator: That's right! You 'watch' the almond for the signs of spring, but I am also at 'watch' over my plans for you, even if you can't see the blooms of my work—yet (Jeremiah 1:11-12).

Watch for the signs, Jeremiah. I am at work, even if you can't see what I'm doing, and I am as faithful as the return of spring. Jeremiah . . . Jeremy . . . . We named the boy after the prophet because God kept asking Jeremiah to do things that made no sense. Jeremy—only God can make sense of this.

chapter 10

INTIMACY

Jeremiah obeyed God even when his commands made absolutely no sense at all. Jeremiah 29:11 says, "'For I know the plans I have for you,' says the LORD. 'They are plans for good and not for disaster, to give you a future and a hope'" (NLT).

You trust in the Lord and rely upon his character, submitting to his commands, believing he is looking out for your best interests.

One day Jesus told the many people following him that only God can give us life in the Kingdom of Heaven: "Human power is of no use at all." He said the only way to enter the Kingdom of Heaven, now and for eternity, was to accept that God does all the work for you; you don't bring any goodness to God (John 6:63-64 TEV).

Because working our way into God's favor appeals to our ego and pride, a number of his followers rejected the Word, slipped to the back of the line, and then snuck away. Jesus looked at the twelve and asked, "What about you? Do you want to leave, too?"

The Bible says Peter answered, "Lord, to whom shall we go? You have the words of eternal life. We have come to believe and to know that you are the Holy One of God" (John 6:68–69 NIV).

Where else can you go? With Jeremy, what were the choices? You can be bitter; you can be angry; you can throw up your hands and walk away from God. What good would that do? Who are you going to blame when it comes to genetics? If you believe God knits each individual in the womb, then it must be his fault.

But if you believe in the character of God, that he loves us and is always looking out for our best interests, then is it possible you can't see everything that he's doing? Jesus always drives us to a choice, and with Jeremy I could see very clearly the utter futility and foolishness of not following after Jesus.

There were some nights and mornings that all I could do to follow Jesus was to lie on my bed and hold my hands up as if I were holding a child up to God and would sing a song that quietly told Jesus he had become the air I breath.

Then, one night, I was alone in the house, studying the Bible in the kitchen and I sensed a presence in the room with me. I knew immediately it was Jesus. And I reacted like we so often do, like Peter wanting to build monuments when Jesus met with Moses and Elijah. I said, "What is it you want,

Lord? Do you want to show me some special scripture?" And I pointed to my Bible.

But then, I felt a touch on my foot, and then both of my feet began to tingle and feel warm—it was almost like someone was washing my feet. And then I sensed Jesus saying, "I don't want you to do anything. I've just come to encourage you. I am with you always." A moment later, the sensation disappeared. I am not Charismatic, but I have no doubt I experienced a moment of Kingdom reality.

——— ——

I used to sell time. You name it, I could deliver.

"Ten seconds? It's yours."

"Five minutes? Would you like that every day of the week?"

"One hour! Tell you what, I'll wrap it with an extra twenty minutes and give it to you for Friday."

I sold advertising on the radio; I could guarantee the hours, minutes, and seconds right there in black and white: "Just sign your John Hancock on the bottom line, and I'll transfer the time to yours from mine."

The only thing is, you had to buy the time before it was spent. Even I didn't have the power to retrieve time-past and assign it to your account. You had to pre-order your blocks of time, and then you had to use 'em or lose 'em.

There are no bargain-bin-remainder sales on time, and that's the brutal truth. I know this because I've spent time searching for one of those sales, and if one could be found, I'm certain I would have found it; and then I would have bought up seconds until they became minutes, minutes until they became hours, hours until they became days, days until they became years, and years until I had a life of time to hand to a young boy named Jeremy.

This, then, is the story of a lifetime measured out in seconds, those silent, persistent ticks that count down until *game over*. No time outs. No two-minute warning. No ability to add extra seconds to the clock.

The advance of the seconds is always there, but some days you're more aware of them than others. No doubt you know those days when one second significantly changes everything in your life, sometimes for good, sometimes for bad, like waiting to hear news from the doctor, and as he speaks, in that one second, your life is radically altered forever with a before and after sequence that reverberates to the depths of your soul.

The seconds slip into focus when the winning goal is scored just as the clock expires; you miss that truck by one tick of the clock because you hesitated when the light turned green; in one second you say the simple words, "I do," and you're transformed from one to two; you hear a deathly rattle and realize it's the last, gasp breath of the one you love.

We manage time, we waste time; we spend time and we save time; we wish the time would come; we wish the time would pass; we see time fly and we feel time drag. We watch clocks and carry calendars, creating the illusion that we somehow control time, and all the while the moments flow forward like a mighty river that cannot be stopped, or harnessed, or re-routed. Any attempts to stop the flow are frustratingly and fatefully futile.

Amidst this flood of seconds, I thought I saw a single moment stop on a stress-filled August morning; I thought for an instant that I could buy more time and hold it forever, like a flint-faced broker riding out a rough market; I thought, perhaps, I could even seal a deal for time-past and put into play some of the wasted time that sits in the cisterns of eternity.

There it is—can you see it?—within the controlled chaos of a hi-tech birthing room; I stand at my wife's side and see our sweet Jeremy for the first time. Cradled in a doctor's hands, his head moves and his belly jostles like a miniature Saint Nick.

He is, as all babies are, a miraculous blend of two meandering lineages, the newest creation from a long line of mixed and matched DNA strands that have transferred traits and characteristics across the centuries. In this one tiny boy is a thousand years of family past and family future.

Jeremy's head is thick with my wife's red hair, looking as if it has been plucked from her very scalp and planted on his. Yet, that same head is unmistakably shaped like mine and my father's and my grandfather's. On both his hands, the little finger curves radically inward, a Walker trait that side-stepped me, but is so pronounced on my older brother's hands that his two outside fingers, when held side-by-side, point in opposite directions.

It has always seemed odd to me that, after months of carrying a child and hours of thanks-a-lot-Eve painful labor—doing the yeoman's work of bringing a baby into the world—the mother is often the last one in the birthing room to actually see the baby. The doctor holds Jeremy up for Sherry to see, and despite her exhaustion and pain—can you see it there, the maternal joy breaking across her face? . . . *may she who gave you birth rejoice!*

I take Jeremy, now wrapped in a blanket, into my arms and I pull him ever so gingerly to my chest. I can feel his warmth, and as I look into his eyes, I recognize the son I have known yet never seen, for we had prayed and played with Jeremy ever since we first became aware that he was living deep within my wife's womb.

For me, that awareness began when I returned from a business trip to find a Father's Day cake sitting on the kitchen table. Sherry and our three-year-old son were extraordinarily excited, and so we cut into the cake and shared slices all around.

My son then handed me a homemade card that read, "Happy Father's Day!"

It was a great card: an instant entry into the refrigerator-door hall of fame, the kind of card that all the king's horses and all the king's forces at Hallmark could only hope to create.

"This is so special," I said. "It means so much to me, and I'm so glad to be your Daddy."

But then I looked at my wife a bit puzzled.

"This is really nice of you both, *but . . .*" I said, drawing out the last word, "Father's Day is still a few months away."

My wife broke into a mischievous smile.

"You didn't look at the card closely enough," she said. "Maybe we should have your reading skills checked, Mr. Editor!"

I gave the card a careful inspection and saw that there were actually two signatures on it: "Love, Christopher and '?'"

And now, gentle reader, follow the flow of time forward—those ticking seconds turning minutes into months—and see me holding the tiny incarnation of that '?.'

My mission in this moment is to place him into the arms of his mother, who takes Jeremy and begins to delicately, preciously re-arrange the blanket in which the boy is wrapped.

A mother and child reunion, Sherry softly introduces herself to Jeremy. She knows this child in so many ways—he's lived inside of her—yet like pen-pal lovers meeting face-to-face, some of the mystery is falling away as if a deep, longing question now receives its answer.

Instinctively, Sherry begins a systematic inspection of the boy's body, like a seasoned curator respectfully examining a once-in-a-life-time find, slowly turning him so she can see the front and back of his head.

She takes his right hand and examines each of his five fingers. She does this by using her own fingers to grasp one of his at a time, gently rolling it around to see it from different angles. All the while, she talks to Jeremy in a low, nurturing voice.

"You have such nice little fingers," she says. "Look at how this one curls; that's something you got from your Daddy."

It's as if she has all the time in the world, this moment expanding like a bubble, swelling larger and larger, stretching toward a burst. It's an illusion, of course, this pregnant pause; the relentless seconds are slip-sliding away like they always do, like they have since God first unleashed the river of time.

Just a few minutes before, we could hear his heartbeat weaken, and my wife sobbed, "Just give me fifteen minutes with him, please God." Then I asked the nurse to disconnect the fetal monitor. We'd been through this before, and we didn't want to hear his diminishing heartbeat if it became a countdown to his death.

He slipped from my wife's body quietly, and his head turned toward me. I thought I was looking at a living, little boy.

I was wrong.

chapter 11

REPUTATION

My youngest son wants to be an actor, so in order to encourage this dream and spend more time with him, I took him to auditions at the local community theatre, where they were casting for "The Homecoming." The play, written by Earl Hamner, Jr. was a precursor to "The Waltons" and eventually became the pilot for the television series.

The scene is set at Christmas Eve and John Walton, who had to travel to another town to find work, is late getting home. A blizzard is coming through and the family is concerned that he may have been in an accident or that he simply won't be able to get through and make it home in time for Christmas.

Since I was, in a sense, starting my life over and was willing to try something new, I asked my son if it would be okay for me to audition for a part. This was his gig, and I didn't want to make him feel as if there was competition between us or that I was pushing in on his "thing." But he said he was okay with it.

To my astonishment, I was cast as Charlie Snead, who drinks too much but also tries to be a good neighbor. He goes hunting illegally to provide the Waltons with a turkey for Christmas dinner. As he says when he drops the turkey off, "Why should people go hungry when there's game a plenty?"

Unfortunately, Charlie gets arrested on Christmas Eve, but before he's taken to jail, the sherriff stops by the local saloon to see if anyone's heard from John Walton. No one will give Charlie a drink, so he laments, "Christmas Eve and I can't get no Coors."

The play became a bittersweet time for me. As we started rehearsals, the divorce had just been finalized and I'd just experienced a layoff. I also knew by then we had to give up the house.

Every night I walked through a play about survival and faith in rural America during the Great Depression. It was a reminder that there was a time when the American people faced few jobs, little money, and a collapsed economy; yet, people still managed to pull together as part of a larger community. Was this nostalgia or true to life?

I remember asking my dad, who was born in 1920, what it was like when he was nine and the Great Depression hit the economy. He said in all seriousness, "We really didn't notice, we were already so poor." If you listen to the gospel music from the Depression era, there was an emphasis on the Kingdom. People were poor, but they were also focused on the eternal, knowing there was more to come and knowing Jesus was leading them there.

Consider the economic problems in the U.S. or, for that matter, the world. The curtain has been pulled back, exposing that the things we put our faith in are not as stable as we think. I wonder if this will help us remember what is really important in life and remind us that life is in Christ. And I wonder if this will lead the church back to serious Kingdom living and the kind of costly discipleship required to follow Christ down the narrow path through the narrow gate.

——— ——

In the novel *The Man Who Was Poe* by Avi, several scenes show Edgar Allan Poe trying to finish a story. He's based the story on the real life events he is experiencing and the boy in the story is based on a real-life boy who asked Poe to help him find his mother.

Poe is often drunk and he begins to have trouble distinguishing between fiction and reality. He keeps getting frustrated because the boy in real life will not submit to his manuscript. He sees the real-life boy as a character in rebellion, a contrary character that Poe will be glad to be done with.

This is often how we approach Christian community. We enter into Christian fellowship with a fantasy of what it should be like. We have an image of how people should act and we try to create them into our image, rather than accepting the reality of who God created them to be. We imagine everyone will be spiritually mature, everyone will get along with each other, everyone will be sensitive to the needs of others, and we'll all love and support each other.

But Bonhoeffer says: "One who wants more than what Christ has established does not want Christian brotherhood. He is looking for some extraordinary social experience which he has not found elsewhere; he is bringing muddled and impure desires into Christian brotherhood."

Our fantasies eat away at the authenticity and transparency required in any Christ-centered fellowship. There's no way others can meet our ideal and so we become frustrated that no one is *acting* like a Christian ought to act.

> "One who wants more than what Christ has established does not want Christian brotherhood. He is looking for some extraordinary social experience which he has not found elsewhere; he is bringing muddled and impure desires into Christian brotherhood."
>
> —BONHOEFFER

The point at which we reach this disillusionment is the point at which we can finally get to the reality of Christ community. We come to Christ broken, knowing we are in desperate need of a Savior, and we must enter Christian fellowship in that same brokenness, understanding that we only enter Christ community through our relationship with Jesus. We are now able to enter our fellowship, "not as demanders but as thankful recipients."

One Sunday night, I stood before the congregation of the church where I was a member and told everyone that God had called me into ministry. The next day, I went to my regular job, but I had this uncertainty about how I should act. I mean, I was called to be a pastor now. Shouldn't I somehow show that by acting differently?

I joked with some friends that I should walk down the hall piously waving at people, saying, "Bless you!" or "Have a blessed day, my friend" or "What's that, you accidentally spray painted my car? You're forgiven, son. Go and be at peace."

But the joke loses its humor if I really do begin acting like I think a pastor should act, and it's just as problematic when the followers of Jesus start acting the way they think followers should act.

Jesus doesn't want you to act like a good person. In fact, he doesn't even want you to be a good person, where you are aware of your own piety. Jesus wants you to be a godly person whose behavior is connected to your intimacy with him and whose service flows from God through Jesus through you to others.

Bonhoeffer says: "All that the follower of Jesus has to do is to make sure that his obedience, following and love are entirely spontaneous and unpremeditated . . . . Otherwise you are simply displaying your own virtue, and not that which has its source in Jesus Christ."

Acting like a follower of Christ has nothing to do with our connection to Christ. In truth, when we start thinking about what we should look like or whom we should impress with Christian behavior, we've changed the very nature of what we're doing. We may do good things and provide noteworthy service, but that doesn't mean it's connected to Jesus and something recognized in the Kingdom of Heaven.

"Genuine love is always self-forgetful in the true sense of the word," says Bonhoeffer. "But if we are to have it, our old man must die with all his virtues and qualities, and this can only be done where the disciple forgets self and clings solely to Christ . . . . The love of Christ crucified, who delivers our old man to death, is the love which lives in those who follow him."

> "Genuine love is always self-forgetful . . . .
> But if we are to have it, our old man must
> die with all his virtues and qualities, and
> this can only be done where the disciple
> forgets self and clings solely to Christ."
>
> —BONHOEFFER

It's unfortunate, Bonheoffer says, that many followers of Jesus get stuck right at this point—at the threshold of the Kingdom but unwilling to die to self. The truth is, the image of the good man or woman easily becomes a form of idolatry because we place that image and our own abilities to be nice above our intimacy with Jesus. We auto-respond from the image instead of talking to our Lord about what we should do or how we should handle a situation.

Jesus had a major problem with the Pharisees because they focused on behavior and image and not on their relationship with the Father. He kept saying, "It starts from the relationship. It starts from the inside and works its way out. You study the Scriptures. Can't you see that?"

So he was blunt and brutal in his criticism of them because they taught others to act like a believer instead of how to be a believer: "How terrible for you, teachers of the Law and Pharisees! You hypocrites! You are like whitewashed tombs, which look fine on the outside but are full of bones and decaying corpses on the inside. In the same way, on the outside you appear good to everybody, but inside you are full of hypocrisy and sins" (Matthew 23:27-28 TEV).

This hypocrisy and idolatry leave us in a state of denial—perhaps the great condition of the modern church—where we act as if we're living the abundant life while secretly living in quiet desperation. The truth is, Bonhoeffer says, we'd rather have a saint in our small group than a sinner because we don't want to deal with the mess. But the problem is, this creates an unsafe environment to bring our problems and our pain, so we all try acting like saints because we're afraid people will see the mess in our own lives.

We end up like people sitting around a fire in a cave but facing outside the circle, seeing the shadows on the walls. And we interact with each other's shadows instead of looking each other directly in the face.

We try to interact with a shadow of Jesus instead of meeting him face-to-face; but he will have none of that. He wants an intimate relationship, and he also has the end game in mind. He has to push us into the reality of the Kingdom so that we can begin learning how to be a citizen there, even as we follow him down the narrow path and through the narrow gate.

I think about the shadows I have seen as a real thing. I think about the shadows of myself that I sometimes project. Images that Jesus is determined "to uproot and to pull down, to destroy and to overthrow, to build and to plant" (Jeremiah 1:10 TEV).

Jesus was a man of no reputation, and I think about what that means in a culture of personal branding.

Later, I found myself alone on Christmas Eve, and I thought about tweeting, "Christmas Eve and I can't get no Coors." Many of my friends would see the humor, but I thought about how that might be misinterpreted among the many others who would read the quote and not understand the context.

chapter 12

COMMUNITY

My wife filed for divorce about two weeks before our twenty-fourth wedding anniversary and it was finalized almost ten months later. During that stressful and frustrating stretch, I was living in the bonus room and stressing over how to provide for my sons and how to be financially fair to my wife. I did not agree with her decision to leave, but I saw no reason to be vindictive. I told her I wanted us both to land on our feet financially.

It wasn't until the day she moved out that I realized I'd been so focused on getting us through this family crisis, I'd given no thought at all to life beyond. But now in a huge, empty house all alone my tears began to flow. I remember yelling to God, "I didn't want this. I never wanted any of this." I sat on the living room floor and, honestly, like a child, I was incapacitated by my tears.

I finally got up, walked around the house, saw the boys' empty rooms, and went back to the same spot in the living room and started crying all over again. Telling the boys about the divorce was the hardest thing I ever had to do, and if I could have taken upon my shoulders the pain they felt that day and will feel for years to come, I would have done so.

My youngest son, not understanding everything, asked me if the divorce meant he'd never get to see me again. It was the only time throughout the divorce that I had to push back a hatred for my wife, pushing those thoughts and feelings to the feet of Jesus.

Over the next few days, I would sit in the same spot in the living room and cry, or I'd walk through the house yelling (in a loving way, of course) at God, making sure he understood my exact situation.

And my situation kept getting worse. After discussing the divorce agreement with four different attorneys, I discovered it was terribly one-sided, with two of them characterizing it as one of the worst they'd ever seen. The bottom line is, I became responsible for all our bills and, by the time I paid for everything, I was left without any money. I don't mean I was left without much money. I mean I had nothing: no reserves, no savings, no CDs, no money market, no retirement accounts.

Then, about three weeks after the divorce, I was laid-off when *Reader's Digest* filed for bankruptcy. Only a year before, having finished my first book and on a flight to the New York City offices of *Reader's Digest*, I thought about the awesomeness of God: when I'd graduated from college so many years before I wanted to write books and work in magazines. My book was published the same week my divorce was finalized.

And so, once again, I trudged through the empty house, praying out loud: "Hey God, I just want to make sure you understand my exact situation."

This is when my fears became tangible. I'd never experienced this before, even though several times I'd stepped out in faith and followed God's prompting to leave a job without having another one lined up. God had always provided almost immediately after taking those steps, but like the disciples, when the Bible says they forgot about the five thousand that Jesus fed, I had lost confidence in the Father's promises. I was free-falling into faithless thinking.

I was afraid I wouldn't be able to pay my bills; I was afraid I wouldn't be able to find another job; I was afraid I wouldn't be able to be productive in another job; I was afraid the court would hold me in contempt because I couldn't pay my wife everything required by the court; I was afraid I'd have to move into someone's basement because I couldn't even afford to rent a small apartment.

I was afraid I was slipping into an inability to function, and what would I do then? I was afraid I'd entered one of those nightmare moments from which you never recover.

I was absolutely and unequivocally overwhelmed. Everything suddenly seemed too complicated, and I was having trouble thinking about what to do. I had to find work, and I had to get the house on the market.

Enter Grace Guthrie. Grace is appropriately named because she embodies God's grace. She chases Jesus with a passion that is far too uncommon today. I didn't even know Grace but God sent her into my life as a realtor and then she became a living picture of Christian community.

Grace would come by just to check on me; she'd call to see how I was doing; she'd stop by to pray with me; she refused to leave me in faithless thinking, continually encouraging me with God's Word, sometimes even rebuking me when I slipped back into thinking someone other than God could be my deliverer.

During this time, God blessed me with the assignment to write the book, *Costly Grace*, based on Bonhoeffer's *The Cost of Discipleship*. This was an amazing gift from God because I was in no condition to write any book proposals, but in this case, the publisher asked me to write the book. And it was a healthy reminder that following Jesus is a call that will cost us everything as we exclusively attach ourselves to him.

I was struggling with juggling everything that needed to be done, from adjusting to a new life to managing my disease to preparing the house for sale. In fact, the thought of prepping the house pushed me deep into depression. I just didn't have the energy to do all the work, but, more so, every item I moved, every closet I opened reminded me of my missing family.

One day Grace, and our mutual friend, Kathy Chapman Sharp, showed up saying they wanted to help set the house up for sale. They walked around discussing ideas, and then Kathy took me down the street to another mutual friend, Donna Stetzer, who did the most amazing thing. She opened the door to her attic and said, "Whatever you need is yours." There was a living room set, a kitchen table, wall hangings, even beds for the boys. She even gave us a Christmas tree.

My son and I were still in the Christmas play, "The Homecoming," and we had the last two shows Sunday afternoon and evening. Grace asked me if she could come by and do some work in the house while we were on stage. I had no idea the magnitude of her plans.

> "If we do not experience others bearing us, then the group we belong to is not Christian. . . . And if anyone refuses to bear another's burden, then he denies the law of Christ."
> —BONHOEFFER

Bonhoeffer says, "God is a God who bears." The Son of God wrapped himself in human flesh and carried the cross and our sins, straight up a hill called Golgotha. We are told to "carry one another's burdens, and in this way you will obey the law of Christ" (Galatians 6:2 TEV). Bearing the burdens of others, says Bonhoeffer, is "precisely what it means to be a Christian." Because we are connected together through Jesus, Bonhoeffer says any burden that threatens to overwhelm one of us should be a burden to all of us. "It is only when he is a burden that another person is really a brother and not merely an object to be manipulated," Bonhoeffer says. We come to see that those who are a burden—who we may label weak—are the very things that make us a community.

Bonhoeffer adds: "If we do not experience others bearing us, then the group we belong to is not Christian. . . . . And if anyone refuses to bear another's burden, then he denies the law of Christ." The law of Christ is that we love one another.

——— ——

When my sons and I arrived home after the play, there were about fifteen people in the house. Grace had brought the high school girls she disciples, some of their friends, and her mother-in-law. Our friend Kathy was there too, and they had done a complete make-over on the house. It did not even look the same; in fact, it looked better than when we had our own furniture in the house. They'd even decorated for Christmas and put up the Christmas tree.

And all around the house I found beautiful home-crafted cards written in an elegant script. When I opened one of the cards, it was one of my devotionals that I'd written to encourage other believers into faithfulness. Grace had taken the time to handwrite about thirty of these cards, each with a different devotional I'd written, and she'd placed them in strategic points around the house.

Knowing how long it took Grace to carefully and beautifully handwrite each note made them a rare treasure to me. And feeding my own words back to me, I think, reflected Peter's example, where he says, "I will always remind you of these matters, even though you already know them and are firmly grounded in the truth you have received" (2 Peter 1:12 TEV).

——— —

An exceptional example of bearing the burdens of another is Samwise Gangee in *The Lord of the Rings* trilogy. Although Frodo gets most of the credit, he never could have completed his journey through Mordor had he not been accompanied by Sam, his loyal and faithful friend.

In truth, Sam is the real hero of the story. He does everything he can to ease his friend's burden, providing sacrificial service through the harshest conditions. Sam listens, he serves, he encourages, and he confronts by speaking the truth in love.

As the two begin to run out of food, Sam eats less in order to give Frodo more. When he realizes they probably won't return from the journey, Sam presses on with Frodo even though he knows it will most likely cost him his own life. When Sam thinks Frodo is dead, he takes the ring intending to finish the journey on Frodo's behalf. When he discovers Frodo is alive, Sam gives the ring back to Frodo, instead of insisting it now belonged to him. In fact, Sam is one of only two people who give the ring up voluntarily (the other one being Frodo's uncle, Bilbo). When Frodo can't go on, Sam picks him up and carries him up a mountain. Sam wasn't concerned about credit, and he never thought twice about sharing Frodo's burden.

> Bonhoeffer says bearing the burdens
> of others is how we become like Christ.
> In fact, this is "precisely what it means
> to be a Christian."

Bonhoeffer says bearing the burdens of others is how we become like Christ. In fact, Bonhoeffer says this is "precisely what it means to be a Christian."

By the way, Sam also shows us that a servant is the hero. Why? Because, in the end, Sam gets the girl.

But I feel more akin to Frodo, who says he wishes the ring had never come to him. He wishes none of this had happened. His friend, Gandalf, says anyone who lives to see such difficult times wishes the same. But they have no choice about facing such times; they only have a choice about what to do with the time they are given. Gandalf says Frodo was meant to take his journey and to carry a burden for others, and he should be encouraged by that.

Oswald Chambers says we may be uncertain of where God will lead us, but we can always be certain he is leading us.

chapter 13

SUFFERING

December comes in cold, and I can't afford to keep the house comfortably warm. At night, I bury myself under two comforters and a couple of blankets. During the day, I wear a hoodie and wrap myself in a blanket. I have gloves with the fingertips cut off so I can type. I drink lots of hot tea and soup.

Kathy tells me I should open the blinds every day to let in the light. It's a strategy for fighting against depression. But when I open the blinds, I see the stark backyard and get depressed anyway.

Out front I see the friends of my youngest son running up and down the cul-de-sac. He would be out there with them, but he doesn't live here anymore. Sometimes they come to the door and ask if my son is there. I wonder if there is a way to put up a court-approved visitation schedule on the mailbox, so they'll know when he's visiting.

I'm still trying to figure out health insurance. No one I try will accept me because my bipolar combined with other conditions gets me eliminated in every initial screening. Someone explains that insurance companies look at bipolar as a disease I will never recover from, that is, there is no cure; at best, it can be managed.

I'm still on a COBRA health insurance extension from a provider based in California, but it's costing me the equivalent of a mortgage payment on an average sized house.

I try AARP, but they shut down my application just like everyone else. My take is the insurance is no different from anyone else; they've just wrapped the AARP brand around it. I cancel my AARP membership, but they keep sending me reminders to join again.

I check out some Christian programs that are not health insurance, but a form of faith, where everybody in the program helps to pay for each other's medical bills. There's a structure to it, so it evens out what you need to contribute each month. But when you get into the fine print, they won't accept people with bipolar into their program.

I think about the time my doctor told me I needed to leave LifeWay Christian Resources. In a sense saying, "Quit your job or destroy your health." I was supposed to slip into a quieter, less stressful life. How could I have lost that message? I think, "Reindeer are brown."

——— ——

Bonhoeffer says God allows suffering because it pulls us deep into his heart. In fact, he sees it as a non-optional step toward spiritual maturity and intimacy with the Father. "Just as Christ maintained his communion with the Father by his endurance, so his followers are to maintain their communion with Christ by their endurance," says Bonhoeffer.

> Bonhoeffer says God allows suffering because it pulls us deep into his heart. In fact, he sees it as a non-optional step toward spiritual maturity and intimacy with the Father.

The truth is, we do not suffer outside the sovereignty and power of God. Whether it is righteous suffering or self-inflicted, God uses suffering to lovingly squeeze out the things out of us that we might otherwise ignore or excuse—the sin, disobedience, and apathy that will get us flagged by security at the gates of the Kingdom of Heaven.

And this is why Jesus so often addresses the weary and brokenhearted. Come to me if you are desperate because only desperate men and women are willing to suffer for my cause. They alone understand God will give them "treasures of darkness and riches from secret places, so that you may know that I, the Lord, the God of Israel call you by your name" (Isaiah 45:3 HCSB).

I stare at an outline of Bonhoeffer's thoughts:

- The cross did not happen to Jesus; it was part of his purpose for coming to earth.

- Suffering does not happen upon me; it is part of God's purpose for my life.
- I can face suffering knowing God uses it to squeeze me into the image of Jesus.
- The cross was not a tragedy for Jesus; it is his greatest glory.
- Just as his suffering was redemptive, God will also use my suffering for good.

Will you help me believe that, Lord?

——— ——

My sister gives me our parent's silver, which had been part of her inheritance. Between the divorce agreement, the most recent lay-off, and paying a hefty mortgage while waiting for the house to sell, I don't have enough money to keep up with the alimony payments. Lori says sell the silver and pay your wife.

I struggle with it emotionally, not ready to give something like that up. Have I really fallen that deeply into a hole? I explained to my wife what I was about to do, and to her credit, she agreed to take less.

Ironically, about this time Conan O'Brien was forced out of the Tonight Show, but NBC was required to pay the show's budget through the last episode. So Conan started a running gag where every night he would spend millions of dollars just to put crazy expensive stuff on his stage. For instance, the show bought the most expensive car in the world, a Bugatti Veyron, then dressed it up like a mouse. And then they limited the car to playing only "Satisfaction" by the Rolling Stones, which jacked up the price because of copyright fees. The total package came to 1.5 million dollars.

I sat every night watching the gag, and I couldn't help but think how Conan could use some of that money to pay off my wife and then give us both houses about two blocks apart. Come on, Conan, put the money into something useful. I then decided I was being selfish, and that I should hope one night Conan would fund Habitat for Humanity (or missions). So Conan, if you happen to read this, I think the Habitat idea is a good one, but if you want to pay off my wife and buy us each a house, I won't turn it down.

——— ——

I'm having trouble focusing. I'm concerned about my productivity. I'm starting to think, "What's the use?" I know this is typical of people with my condition, but I do things like go to the grocery store and after putting one or two things in the cart, I am overcome with what I call depressive sleep. I know my energy and ability to function outside my house is running down like sand in an hourglass, so I leave the store, knowing I'll have to try again tomorrow.

The human mind is an amazing and fragile thing. When my mother was slipping into an Alzheimer's mixed-up reality, she once thought I was my dad, and she was so happy I'd finally come to take her home. Another time, she greeted me warmly but wanted to know why I was there. As the conversation progressed, I knew exactly where she was. She was in the Officer's

Club at Forbes Air Force Base, enjoying lunch after church. But that was thirty years before and I would have been only six years old, but she accepted me as an adult in that memory.

> Bonhoeffer reminds me that we live in delusions of our own self-righteousness, of this life being all of life, of Jesus being an add-on to our lives.

One of the most difficult things I've ever had to deal with was telling her that her sister had died. She cried deeper and heavier than any time I had seen before. But the next day, she didn't remember, and so I had to tell her again, and she cried again. On the third day, I had to tell her again because I knew the petition was the only way she'd remember. Finally, on the fourth day, she greeted me quietly and said, "I know Audrey is dead."

Bonhoeffer, again, reminds me that we live in delusions of our own self-righteousness, of this life being all of life, of Jesus being an add-on to our lives.

———

It's New Year's and I think about my parents meeting at a church watch night service in 1936, when they were both sixteen years old. They stayed together for the rest of their lives, well over fifty years, until my father died.

I think about my father's parents, who decided to get married at nineteen while riding on a streetcar home from church, so they got off and went to find the justice of the peace. Then, they walked to my great-grandmother's home and announced they were married. My great-grandmother burst into tears, but my grandparents stayed together the rest of their lives, well over fifty years, until she died.

I think about my mother's parents, who grew up in such a small town in Mississippi that there were only two girls in my grandfather's senior class. He asked my grandmother to marry him, and then she helped him write a gracious letter to the other girl, letting her know he was going to marry Rogenia. They stayed together the rest of their lives, well over fifty years, until she died.

I'm having serious writer's block and can't get my manuscript written. If it weren't for the daily encouragement and practical support of my friend, Mark Kelly, I wouldn't make any progress on the manuscript. Although I've wanted to write books my whole life, I'm so discouraged that I decide that, once I finish the manuscript, I'll give up writing for good.

Jeremiah kept trying to quit. He finally told God, "You seduced me into this. You never told me it would be this hard." God refused to coddle Jeremiah. He said, "You wanted the anointing. I'm giving you the anointing. Now get back to work."

I think about a night when a pain hit me so suddenly and severely that it felt like someone had just kicked me between the legs. I grabbed my wife's hand and she said I almost broke it. The next morning, I walked into my doctor's office, standing erect and quickly telling him about the pain. He was perplexed, but after a quick blood test, he told me I had a perforated appendix. He said, "What threw me off is that I have never seen anyone walking erect after the appendix ruptures."

How far do you go until you can't go any further?

chapter 14

COINCIDENCE

Do you think there is such a thing as coincidence?

In Kingdom reality, there simply cannot be. Random doesn't happen in the Kingdom. Oswald Chambers says God is the Great Engineer, creating circumstances to bring about moments in our lives of divine importance, leading us to divine appointments.

Was it a coincidence that Jesus came upon the woman at the well? Was it a coincidence that Peter, doing what Jesus told him to do, pulled a fish from the Sea of Galilee that held in its mouth a coin for paying taxes?

Was it a coincidence that a caravan to Egypt came by just as Joseph's brothers were about to kill him, so they sold him into slavery instead? Was it a coincidence that years later Joseph, now a powerful leader in Egypt, would save his brothers from starvation?

Was it a coincidence that Caesar Augustus decreed that a census should be taken of the entire Roman world, sending Joseph and Mary to Bethlehem just in time for Jesus to be born according to prophecy?

Jesus says God actively works within our circumstances. "It is not our judgment of the situation which can show us what is wise," says Bonhoeffer. "But only the truth of the Word of God. Here alone lies the promise of God's faithfulness and help."

In other words, we must leave it up to God to interpret our circumstances. Only he is capable of understanding all the facts and only he sees the significance of every detail.

> "It is not our judgment of the situation which can show us what is wise. But only the truth of the Word of God. Here alone lies the promise of God's faithfulness and help."
>
> —BONHOEFFER

This pushes us to another choice for or against Jesus: Is God involved in your circumstances or not?

There was a day when I realized I would not be able to make my next mortgage payment, so I talked to God about my circumstances. I was tired of the financial pressure, but what else could I do but move forward? "God, I don't know what to do, but I'm looking to you. I haven't got a clue."

Although I'd applied for several jobs, I hadn't received a single call back. You could argue I have an impressive resume, but it is a highly niched one. I'd been in ministry more than twenty years, but where do I fit in business? I had two graduate degrees, but the mixture of coursework qualified me to teach only theology and not the things I probably was more qualified by experience to teach, like writing.

As a divorced Southern Baptist pastor, I was disqualified from most church positions. Only about 4 percent of all Southern Baptist pastors are divorced. And I was no longer qualified for some of the high-level ministry positions I'd held in the past, such as when I was editor-in-chief of a nationally distributed family magazine.

It didn't matter because I was coming to the realization that I could no longer handle the stress of those jobs or a pastorate because of my bipolar disorder. I'd always been a highly productive worker, but my confidence was collapsing and I wasn't sure if I could handle a standard forty-hour-a-week job.

I was picking up freelance work, but I was having trouble concentrating and it pushed me towards depression because I was angry with some of the things I had to do to make money. I had one of my yelling sessions with God (I'm so glad he allows that), reminding him that I'd paid my dues. I didn't want to go back to writing basic news stories and press releases. The empty house let me vent my anger, and then I'd quiet down and say, "Okay God, whatever you want. You're in charge."

By then, I was having out-loud conversation with God. There was no one else to talk to in the house. One day I said, "You know, God. I really like working on Rick Warren's e-magazine (something I helped Rick launch about eight years before). And that's the kind of job I need right now, where I can work around my energy levels. Do you think you can find something like that for me to do?"

A few days later, the phone rang. It was my friend, David Chrzan, chief of staff at Saddleback Church.

He said, "Jon, we have a staff member leaving, and I wanted to see if you could help us with some on-line work for a while?"

chapter 15

GOD'S TIMING

When we put our house in California up for sale, the housing market was stalling, and we were concerned about losing money or not being able to sell. The mortgage was huge. The house sold to the first family to look at it.

There are all kinds of reasons houses sell quickly or take a long time to sell, but I've always been particularly attentive to Christians who put a house on the market because they are responding to God's call.

I've watched as those houses sell the same day they're listed but I've also seen them take forever to sell, forcing the families to pay for a place to live while still paying the mortgage on an empty house. One of my friends, after waiting two years for his house to sell, eventually donated it to a non-profit organization, getting him out from under the monthly payment, even though he lost all his equity.

Yet, I believe in God's economy and that means he can sell any house at any time he desires.

So why is there sometimes a huge delay? Because God's goal is to get us focused on Kingdom thinking and Kingdom finances. As Bonhoeffer teaches, God is continually pushing us into places where we can develop more faith, places where we must make a choice between trusting him and leaning on our own understanding. And Bonhoeffer notes, these are always choices for or against Jesus

What about my friend whose house now belongs to a non-profit? Perhaps God was pushing him into a Shadrach, Meshach, and Abednego moment where his faith took him to the place he could say, "Even if he doesn't rescue me, he is still my God."

Perhaps God delays because he wants us desperately looking for him and how he provides, helping us to develop the faithful attitude of gratefulness.

When my wife and I were preparing to go to seminary, we put our condominium in Florida up for sale. The bottom had dropped out of the condo market and several of our neighbors were having trouble attracting buyers or selling at a loss of five to ten thousand dollars (which seems so acceptable, now that I've lost over $100,000).

We didn't even have $1,000 to lose back then, so I was praying about that but stressing over the thought that the condo simply wouldn't sell. "God, don't you want us to go to seminary?" God pushed me toward Kingdom thinking, reminding me he could sell the condo anytime he wanted. "But right now I want you to bloom where you are planted."

And then he guided me to Jeremiah 29. Many of us are familiar with Jeremiah 29:11: "I alone know the plans I have for you, plans to bring you prosperity and not disaster, plans to bring about the future you hope for."

But that verse is actually part of a "Letter from God" to the Jewish people who are being held captive in Babylon. They want to go home to Israel, but God says it isn't time yet. He tells them, "Build houses and settle down. Plant gardens and eat what you grow in them. Marry and have children. Then let your children get married, so that they also may have children. You must increase in numbers and not decrease. Work for the good of the cities where I have made you go as prisoners. Pray to me on their behalf, because if they are prosperous, you will be prosperous too" (Jeremiah 29:5-7 TEV).

God says it's going to be a while, so make a life. Don't invest your energy in hopes of leaving; instead, invest your energy in the people around you. Don't be physically present but mentally somewhere else, thinking of the future or the past, thinking of someplace else. Following Jesus requires that we be fully present *in the present.*

God also says pray for the place you live, because as it prospers, you will prosper. He says, ". . . Seek me, and you will find me because you will seek me with all your heart" (Jeremiah 29:13 TEV).

It seemed God was saying that when we left for seminary— this year, next year, or in ten years—was totally up to him. So my wife and I decided to take a break from that need to have your house look perfect when it is on the market, and we took down the "For Sale" sign. And we began to invest our time in the people around us, and we jumped back into serving at church, no longer hesitant because we thought we'd be moving in a few months.

About three months later, I got a call from a realtor who went to our church. He said, "Are you still trying to sell your condo?" I said, "We'd like to, but we've taken it off the market for now." He said, "I have a buyer."

And within a few days, the condominium had sold. Instead of taking a loss, we walked away with $84 in our pocket, plus the money required to buy a brand new washer and dryer, something that had been very important to my wife. God be praised!

—— —

When my family came back from California, we had plans to find a great house with a great backyard, one we could live in while the boys grew up. We never intentionally changed from that objective; we just lost perspective, bit by bit. C. S. Lewis says you never talk a man out of what he believes; he just forgets a little bit at a time. It's easy to forget that we're in a life and death struggle, not against each other, but against the real enemy, Satan, who is truly working to destroy us. Paul reminds us, "This is no afternoon athletic contest that we'll walk away from and forget about in a couple of hours. This is for keeps, a life-or-death fight to the finish against the Devil and all his angels" (Ephesians 6:12 MSG).

Bonhoeffer adds: "When all is said and done, the life of faith is nothing if not an unending struggle of the spirit with every available weapon against the flesh. How is it possible to live the life of faith when we grow weary of prayer, when we lose our taste for reading the Bible, and when sleep, food and sensuality deprive us of the joy of communion with God?"

Looking back, God gave several warnings not to buy at all, let alone a more expensive and larger house than we would normally purchase, but we weren't focused on listening. We failed to follow the approach we'd taken so many times before—trusting God has that one specific house picked out for us, and if we couldn't find it in our timeline, then God was working off his own timeline. Kingdom thinking, Kingdom economy, Kingdom calendar.

> "When all is said and done, the life of faith is nothing if not an unending struggle of the spirit with every available weapon against the flesh. How is it possible to live the life of faith when we grow weary of prayer, when we lose our taste for reading the Bible, and when sleep, food and sensuality deprive us of the joy of communion with God?"
> —BONHOEFFER

My wife and I were having far too many dishwasher dialogues; our attempts at counseling had broken down; and any real communication between us had shut down. Any fool will tell you, this is an excellent time to make a major purchase, like buying a house.

But I also think I was sicker than I realized. All the stress from California, the move, my marriage, living in small apartments, and the uncertainty of our financial future was draining me to dangerous levels—not taking the battery down low to where it takes a little longer to recharge, but taking it down to such a low level that it was in danger of not being able to recharge.

I was back to sleeping for hours because it was a refuge from the stress and confusion I felt. I was having trouble working and concentrating, doing my job in coffee shops and in the backseat of my car. It was difficult to stay focused in the apartment; I was desperate for some stability, which included the sense of permanency in a home and a permanent place to work.

I didn't know how serious my disease was and that I was entering a lethargic state that fogged my thinking and detached me from consequences—the cause-and-effect of confused thinking and bipolar behavior. Since then I've learned that people with bipolar II are at greater risk for suicide, partly because we swing down lower than other bipolar designations, but also because we are more effective at it. We tend to use more lethal means.

So now I'm living in a virtually empty house watching a discouragingly small parade of people walk through to see if it's the right house for them. There are so many other houses on the market now that are available for twenty-five or thirty percent less than they were not a year ago, and the market is still in a tailspin. It seems as if the value of my house is dropping every week.

And I hate feeling as if I can't live in my own house. Everything has to stay neat in case someone wants to see the house and I am in such a critical state that I don't want to say no to anyone.

Once again I am living and working like a nomad, with things I need on a regular basis stacked in laundry baskets, so I can throw them in the car and go work in a coffee shop whenever my realtor needs to bring a potential buyer to the house.

A couple comes by to look a second time and they've brought other people from their church. They stay a long time praying through the house and asking God if it was the right home for them. I see the humor in the situation: I am praying God would show them it is the right house for them; but I then did what I knew I was supposed to do, and asked God to guide them to the right house, whether it was mine or someone else's.

The thing about that prayer was that it helped me too, because when they did not buy my house, I could say quietly to myself, "Go in peace, and know God's hand is guiding you."

Paying the mortgage each month was draining away what little money I had left. I determined that I couldn't go past April, and I got a sense from God that it would sell, but he and I would ride it out until April. *What else can I do, Lord, but follow you. There is nowhere else to go.*

Finally, one family came and agreed to buy the house. I started making plans to move, but I had a check in my spirit, and so did Grace. About a week later, the family asked to be let out of their contract. I was numb and like King Hezekiah, I told God, "I don't know what to do, but I'm looking to you."

What choice did I have but to move forward in faith? My anger wasn't going to sell the house or convince anyone to buy it. In fact, the Bible says man's anger will not bring about God's righteousness.

Then about a week later, the same family came back. They wanted the house and we closed on April 14.

chapter 16

PROVISION

When you're living in an empty house, starting all over again, you'll find yourself stressing over things you never expected. For me, it was a washing machine.

I'd lived forever with a washer and dryer in my house, and suddenly the utility room was empty. There's something to be said about the convenience of throwing things into the washer, and then going to do other things without being tied down for the time of the cycle. It's a freedom taken for granted until you're forced to plan trips to the laundromat. I found myself wearing just about everything I had in my closet so I could lengthen the time before I had to go back.

When someone would invite me to their house, I'd show up with a laundry basket and ask if I could do a load. Yes, there's nothing better to spark conversation than to sit around waiting for the dryer cycle to end.

Many times my friend, Kathy, let me use her washer and dryer, but God worked through her in a surprising and significant way. One day she told me she thought she'd found a place for me to live. My house was still on the market, and I knew I didn't have enough money to rent an apartment once I left.

She connected me with David and Susan Moffitt, a couple who are totally submitted to Jesus. They had moved into a new house, but wanted to keep their old house. It was like an old homestead and it meant a great deal to them.

They were letting someone live in the house, but that person would be leaving soon, and Susan suggested I drive by to see if I'd be interested in living there. She said, "It's a little rough, but if any house has character, this one has it."

So I drove through a neighborhood of older, upscale homes, down a street lined with trees, creating the kind of entrance effect you might find as you enter the grounds to an old Southern college. Way down at the end of the road, I could see a white house with a white picket fence. It looked as if it was sitting in the middle of the road, but, as I got closer, I could see it was a visual effect because the road took a sharp turn to the right just in front of the house.

Surrounded by upscale homes and across a lake from million dollar homes, the Moffitt house was the last holdout from the parceled progress that turned a planation and some farms into a model of the good life associated with the American dream. The Moffitt house was an older structure, perhaps from the 1940s. It looked like a farmhouse and sat on an acre or two.

I pulled into the dirt and gravel driveway that made a circle to and from the house and drove up to the front, next to the white picket fence.

Just as I stopped the car, three deer walked out from behind a large bush and stood a few feet from me on the driveway. And, I kid you not, right on cue, Amy Grant's version of I'll Be Home For Christmas" started playing on the radio. I knew right then that this was God's plan for me.

Later, I called Susan and told her I'd like to walk toward moving into the house. I hesitated, and then I asked, "How much are you planning to charge?" She said, "Oh, we weren't planning to charge anything. We're glad if we can bless you."

There is significance to that moment that goes beyond the fact that I had a place to live. I would say it was the moment when I finally placed my foot firmly on the waters of faith, sure of what I hope for, certain of what I do not see. And I can see Jesus in David and Susan Moffitt.

It also reached deep into me, to a place buried underneath the shattered, idolatrous image of a nice guy. I had held onto the belief that people are basically good, that they would do the right thing when push came to shove. It is a romantic image many of us carry, even though it is an unbiblical belief. It is sentimental foolishness. And through the divorce I lost my faith in people, and maybe that is a good thing because Jesus says there is only one who is good.

My faith was misdirected. I tried to be a good guy, instead of a godly one. And I expected others, even non-believers, to be good people too. But I know the darkness that can invade my own heart, and if I cannot be trusted to always be other-centered, then why should I expect it of other people, especially those who do not have the Holy Spirit working within them?

"Can't we all just get along" won't work because humans are incapable of pulling that off. Only God can transform our hearts, and only Jesus can push us into places of otherness.

> "It is only by living completely in this world
> that one learns to live by faith."
>
> —BONHOEFFER

But he has to do that in this fallen world. Bonhoeffer says: "It is only by living completely in this world that one learns to live by faith." Jeremiah is blunt with the Babylonian exiles, telling them that God arranged for them to be in crisis, so he could push them to the very edge of existence, and only there will they be able to focus solely on God and his Kingdom.

——— ——

David Moffitt met me at the house and it was as charming on the inside as the out. It had uneven wooden floors, a kitchen gloriously devoid of marble counters, and a floor plan from the days when we still thought houses should be utilitarian, not show places or investments—simply homes. Susan was absolutely right. The house had character, a sense of home, refuge, and God's peace.

David and I agreed I could stay for at least six months, and that I pay for utilities, make repairs, and cut the grass. I was to become a steward of their property, and I saw that as a good reminder that I am simply a steward of all God gives me.

As we talked, David took me through a door at the back of the kitchen onto a wooden sun porch. There, at one end, I saw a washer and dryer.

God provides for our needs and he is never stingy in how he gives.

chapter 17

PRAYER

Living alone for the first time in my life, I wanted a dog, so I asked God to give me one. He said, "Will you feed her and clean up her messes?" "Oh, yes, Heavenly Father, you know I will. Please, please, please let me get a dog."

Bonhoeffer says our conversations with God should be casual, like a child talking to a parent. "If God were ignorant of our needs, we should have to think out beforehand *how* we should tell him about them, *what* we should tell him, and whether we should tell him or not. Thus faith, which is the mainspring of Christian prayer, excludes all reflection and premeditation," says Bonhoeffer.

I wanted a dog for companionship, but I also knew a dog helps someone with bipolar because feeding and walking it helps to create some structure and routine throughout the day. But, for the first time in my life, I was uncertain if I could even afford a dog, particularly keeping up with the shots and veterinarian visits that would be required.

> "If God were ignorant of our needs, we should have to think out beforehand how we should tell him about them, *what* we should tell him, and whether we should tell him or not. Thus faith, which is the mainspring of Christian prayer, excludes all reflection and premeditation."
>
> —BONHOEFFER

So I listened to Bonhoeffer, who says, "The right way to approach God is to stretch out our hands and ask of One who we know has the heart of a Father." He says our prayers can be spontaneous and confident because they are based on our faith that God will hear and answer them, not on the words we say or the form of prayer we use.

And Jesus is the proof that God wants such intimacy with us. He is our bridge to God, and we become intimate with the Father through Jesus. With that in mind, I prayed a simple prayer, but also one that was specific. "Father, I would like a dog, and this is what I think I need:

- One that is hypoallergenic, because I am allergic to dogs that shed. I'd really like a cockapoo—a cross between a cocker spaniel and poodle.

- One that is older and already trained.
- One that is female, because my last dog was a very territorial male.
- One that is around thirty pounds.
- One that I can afford to keep."

About two weeks before the house sold, I sensed God telling me to look online for a dog. I remember saying, "God, it's still too soon." But, still in remedial obedience class, I did what God said to do, and started looking for rescue dogs online.

I found a dog that seemed to fit my criteria at a place just around the corner from my house called "The Hairy Moose." I walked the dog around for a while, but there just didn't seem to be a connection. When I returned the dog, the woman at the front desk asked, "What are you looking for?"

I said, "I really was hoping to find a cockapoo."

She said, "Just a minute, there was someone who called the other day with a cockapoo." She looked around the desk and finally found a 3 x 5 index card with information about the dog.

The woman said, "She called a few days ago, but we haven't had time to process her. Give her a call and see if she has the right dog for you."

I called Laura West, who owned Pumpkin, a four-year-old female cockapoo, who weighed around thirty pounds. Laura loved Pumpkin, but she was on the road all the time and didn't want the dog to spend long days alone in an apartment.

A lot of people today want "re-homing" fees for their dogs, trying to recoup some of what the dog has cost them. When I asked Laura how much she wanted for Pumpkin, she said, "I just want her to have a good home!" She also told me Pumpkin was current on all her shots.

After meeting Pumpkin, I could tell she was a gift from God, and I told Laura about how I'd prayed specifically for this dog. And I think that blessed Laura, because she is a believer, too.

(My youngest son started off with reddish hair, and so, when he was little, I would call him "Pumpkin." We decided to give the dog, Pumpkin, a middle name, and so we now call her Jasmine.)

——— ——

There is an old, unused barn near the edge of the Moffitts' property and various critters, such as possums and raccoons, come and go from there. There are also two turkey vultures that live in the barn and spend most of their day hanging out in the loft doors at the front of the barn. Their gaze follows Jasmine and me with a nonchalant twist of the neck meant to hide a sinister eye.

Jasmine knows it is wrong to go near the old barn, but she saw a black cat run behind there and took off for a playful chase. Unfortunately, it wasn't a cat. It was a skunk, and Jasmine was quite surprised to get a face full of stink. She smelled so bad I didn't even want to bring her into the house; I sequestered her in the bathroom while I figured out how to get her clean.

I found several home remedies for removing skunk stink on the Internet. The recipes called for ingredients such as tomato juice or a mixture of hydrogen peroxide and baking soda, and I think one listed dark chocolate (okay, I made that up—the dark chocolate was for me).

These mixtures removed the bite of the skunk stink (an eye-watering, garlic-like perfume) but the overall smell was still there. By then it was almost midnight, so I took an old blanket, put it on the floor of the bathroom, and let poor Jasmine spend the night there.

The next morning, I went to the pet store and found a remarkable de-skunker that removed every bit of the stink and left Jasmine smelling wonderfully clean.

I share this story because it helps illustrate what Jesus has done for you. The Bible says, "But God has shown us how much he loves us—it was while we were still sinners that Christ died for us!" (Romans 5:8 TEV).

Jasmine knew she was forbidden from going near the barn, but temptation appeared in the form of (what she thought) was a black cat. Sin is always deceptive, and it always costs more than we think it will. Jasmine thought she'd have some fun; instead, she ended up with the stink of sin all over her.

I still loved Jasmine and wanted her to come into the house with me, but I couldn't let her have the run of the house while she carried the stink of sin. She needed to be cleansed; otherwise, the stink would permeate my home.

That's how God views our sin. He can't let us back into heaven until we're cleansed from our sin; otherwise, our sin would stink up the whole place. Jesus came to cleanse us from our sin, and his bloody sacrifice washes us whiter than snow (Psalm 51:7). When we confess our sin and obediently trust

Jesus, we can walk confidently into God's home, knowing he will welcome us as his daughters and sons.

If, when we were at our worst, we were put on friendly terms with God by the sacrificial death of his Son, now that we're at our best, just think of how our lives will expand and deepen by means of his resurrection life! (Romans 5:10).

——— ——

We are called to bear the sins of others just as Jesus bore our sins. We bear the sins of others when we forgive them, regardless of what their sin costs us. We bear the sins of others when we're willing to pick them up and carry them home, even if it means we will have to sacrifice for helping them.

Jasmine's disobedience cost me. I was taking her out for a quick walk before going to bed, but I suddenly faced the major project of getting Jasmine clean. By the time I got her into the bathroom, the smell was on my clothes, in my nose, and smeared into a towel I'd wrapped around her. I was fortunate the skunk's smell didn't permeate the whole house.

Was the "skunked up" towel I threw away worth more than my dog? Of course not! Was the sleep I lost worth more than my dog? Of course not! Were the divine privileges Jesus gave up to bear the costs of your sins worth more than bringing you home to the Father? Of course not! Jesus knows you are worth every bit of his sacrifice.

We pay a cost when we help others find freedom in Christ. Dietrich Bonhoeffer says bearing the sins of others, even when it means suffering and rejection, creates the distinction between "an ordinary human life and a life committed to Christ."

The truth is, as we follow Jesus down the narrow path, he will lovingly and ruthlessly place us on the anvil of his grace and then hammer us into the shape of Christ. When we retreat from this Kingdom reality, we back into the shadows of our finite thinking. For instance, Peter thinks he is doing the right thing when he tries to stop Jesus from going to the cross, but what he actually is doing is attempting to force his own false sense reality onto the Lord. Peter insists that Jesus fit into his image of the Messiah.

> As we follow Jesus down the narrow path, he will lovingly and ruthlessly place us on the anvil of his grace and then hammer us into the shape of Christ.

In fact, Bonhoeffer says Jesus must not only suffer; he must also be rejected because a suffering messiah may appear to the world as something heroic but a rejected messiah takes the halo of glory away from the passion. All the glory goes to God and the focus becomes the resurrection of Christ, not the gallant death of a martyr.

The cost of discipleship, then, is this: The way we become like Jesus is through suffering and rejection. Jesus became the Christ because he was rejected and suffered, and for us to become his disciples—to become like Christ—we must share in his suffering and rejection.

In fact, Jesus says we are blessed when we are persecuted (rejected) for doing the things he requires of us. This proves we are citizens of the Kingdom of Heaven (Matthew 5:10). Is it possible that one of the reasons so many of us are stuck at the threshold of Christian maturity is that we fear rejection and that keeps us from becoming more like Jesus?

——— ——

When we're inside the yard, I sometimes walk Jasmine without a leash. She's very good at responding to the command, "Come"—*most of the time.* When I call her, she usually responds right away, but sometimes she's caught up in a particular scent and so she comes in stages. I know she hears me because she takes a quick look at me, then she goes back to sniffing, weighing in her mind whether she should respond right away or keep tracking down her temptation.

Bonhoeffer stresses again and again that, when we do not respond immediately to the commands of Jesus, we are in disobedience. Regardless of how we think we can behave, we are not in a debate with God's Word, Jesus Christ. God gives us the free will to decide how we will respond to him, but that doesn't mean our choice changes the reality of God's sovereignty.

His Word speaks, we respond. It is as simple as that. When we keep sniffing around after we've received the command, we're nothing more than disobedient. Jasmine provides an example of how, as Bonhoeffer notes, we reinterpret God's commands for our convenience, believing we can somehow wrestle the reality of God's universe into the mythology of our faithless world.

God tells us to come, but we think, "What he really means is that I must start sniffing in a different direction." Or, "What he really means is I must stay within the yard, but I don't really have to actually come over to him."

In this way, we create the very confusion that then has us throwing up our hands, blaming God because we can't figure out what he wants us to do. We play "Where's Waldo" with God, looking for the red and white striped answer somewhere in the chaos of life, seldom looking up to Kingdom reality and realizing God is holding the book open for us with a finger pointing to the answer to our prayers.

Our faith is tied to our obedience to Jesus, an obedience that leads us into an intimate trust with God's Word. When the disciples ask Jesus to give them more faith, he says, in essence, "You're missing the point. There is no 'more or less' when it comes to faith. In fact, if you had faith so small it could be compared to the size of a tiny seed, that would be enough to move mountains."

"The real point is obedience. You're faith becomes stronger by doing what the Word tells you to do. You're thinking like a servant who works all day and then expects to be commended as if he'd done above and beyond what was required. You're obedience is required—it's all part of a day's work. But that is how your faith will catch the wind of Kingdom power" (based on Luke 17:5-13, some language suggested by The Message paraphrase).

One day, as Jasmine and I are walking around the property, I hear a noise and look up. There is a turkey vulture sitting in a branch about twenty feet directly above us. It tilts its neck, gives me an ominous stare, and flutters its wings with a sound like an ill wind blowing in.

chapter 18

POSSESSIONS

After my wife moved out, I started looking at all the things I would have to replace—basic things I thought I needed, such as dishes and utensils. But I didn't have any money, and I was afraid to spend what little I had.

But I also knew I'd been in dozens of garages where people had old dish sets and cooking utensils sitting off on some shelf. So I started asking around and ended up with a hodge-podge collection of dishes and cups. They were perfectly functional and I was grateful just to have plates to eat on.

The only things I purchased were a frying pan and an ornery toaster oven that burns toast no matter what setting it's on. Clearly, I wasn't cooking fancy, but I was meeting my needs and feeding the boys when they were with me.

When I moved out of the house, almost everything I owned ended up stacked tightly in a storage unit about the size of a one-car garage. And the thing is, most of the stuff stacked there was junk. It was the kind of stuff that eventually finds its way into the back of the closet, or the bottom drawer, or a corner of the garage.

Jesus says our true life—our life in the Kingdom—has nothing to do with the things we own. No matter how much we accumulate, we can never turn it into real life (Luke 12:15). But is our desire for bigger garages, garden garages, three-car garages, and storage units much different from the rich man who built bigger barns never thinking about his future, about eternity, about the chance he might die sooner than later?

My mother had me thinking about this a few years ago, long before the divorce. When her Alzheimer's progressed to the point we had to move her out of her home, my sister and I were overwhelmed by the amount of stuff my parents had accumulated. Sure, there was some nice furniture and jewelry, but so much of it had no value beyond their death. And so much of it could have been given away or thrown away years before.

And you know how garage sales go—people are looking for bargains. The thing you paid $400 for is only worth $10. The furniture that created a comfortable and stylish living room is now just used pieces to sell, or divide, or give away—to dispose of in some way. The kitchen table that nearly defines your childhood doesn't sell because everyone else sees it as an old piece of junk.

But then there is junk all over the place, in the closets, in the drawers, in the garage. And it's worth nothing, and must not have been worth much to my parents because it hasn't been used for years and years.

I think about all I've lost, but the junk still remains. I think that maybe this mid-life strip down is a blessing in disguise because it clears away many of my possessions and re-defines what is important. My sons won't have to close out a cluttered house like my sister and I had to for my parents. When I pack a box for Goodwill, I tell my oldest son, "I'm doing this for you." He looks at me, not sure what I mean. "I'm getting rid of this now, so you won't have to when I die."

And isn't that the way of the Kingdom? Why do we keep things with the intent of giving them away when we die? Can we enjoy them for a season and then pass them on? Recently, I talked to a friend of mine while he was sitting in his living room gathering things to give his children. He'd just lost his house to the bank, and he had to clear everything out. He said, "You know, the kids were going to get this anyway. Now I get the joy of giving it to them while I am alive."

In God's economy, he gives us things, not so we can stuff them in storage but so we can use them to bring him glory and advance his Kingdom. One way we're meant to use the things God gives us is to bless others through them, or God may give something to us so we can give it to someone else.

Bonhoeffer says: "The way to misuse our possessions is to use them as an insurance against the morrow. Anxiety is always directed to the morrow, whereas goods are in the strictest sense meant to be used only for today. By trying to ensure for the next day we are only creating uncertainty today."

In other words, when we stuff our garages and storage units with things we could be giving to others—and we do this in case we have a need in the future—then we're declaring something other than God provides for our security. Why not trust God when the need arises?

> "The way to misuse our possessions is to use them as an insurance against the morrow. Anxiety is always directed to the morrow, whereas goods are in the strictest sense meant to be used only for today. By trying to ensure for the next day we are only creating uncertainty today."
>
> —BONHOEFFER

Does this mean we can't have some savings or buy extra light bulbs? You have to ask Jesus that question and that's the point. We gather and collect without ever asking Jesus what we should do, or why he is providing more than we need. Perhaps it is for a future need, or perhaps it is to give away.

It leads to a cycle of always putting off our total abandonment to Jesus. We think, "When I get this much in the bank, then I'll focus more on ministry. If I could just get a bigger house, then I'll be able to host a small group in my home."

And that leads to scenarios where we are unable to respond to Jesus because we're weighted down with too much stuff. We're unable to do the ministry Jesus calls us to do because we have to work extra hours to pay for the things we have. We sense Jesus telling us to step out in faith to pursue a different career, one that matches the way he has shaped us for ministry—but then we think, "I can't quit my job, Jesus! I have a mortgage to pay."

How do we know the difference between the things we need to keep for legitimate use and those that represent an unnecessary accumulation of possessions?

> "Everything which hinders us from loving God above all things and acts as a barrier between ourselves and our obedience to Jesus is our treasure, and the place where our heart is."
> —BONHOEFFER

Bonhoeffer says we only need to reverse the words of Jesus: the place you will most want to be and end up being is the place where your treasure is. Small or large, Bonhoeffer says, "Everything which hinders us from loving God above all things and acts as a barrier between ourselves and our obedience to Jesus is our treasure, and the place where our heart is."

The more we possess, the more we have to care for our possessions, and that leads to our possessions eventually possessing us. Jesus doesn't forbid us to have possessions. His point is that we should not allow our possessions to get in the way of following him—and the more we accumulate, the more likely we are to worry about how we will pay for, take care of, keep and protect the things we own.

Suddenly, we're serving things instead of serving Jesus. We begin to believe, "It is all up to me to pay for these things and to provide for my needs and my family's needs." And that is fallen thinking locked into the economy of this world. Jesus says that in God's economy, in the Kingdom of Heaven, our Father is the provider and he knows our needs better than we do ourselves. *Look around; look at how he provides. Now believe he will provide for you.*

Bonhoeffer says: "It is senseless to pretend that we can make provision because we cannot alter the circumstances of this world. Only God can take care, for it is he who rules the world. Since we cannot take care, since we are so completely powerless, we ought not to do it either. If we do, we are dethroning God and presuming to rule the world ourselves."

After two years, I am amazed at how little I have had to replace. I just don't need stuff. And when someone gives me a gift certificate to a store, I find myself walking down the aisles and having trouble figuring out what to buy because I don't want to add to my junk. I don't want to buy anything I don't really need.

I did finally buy one luxury item. I could have kept scraping burnt toast and throwing away dishes the ornery toaster oven seasoned with carbon.

But I decided to splurge and buy a new toaster.

chapter 19

REGRETS

God has blessed us with two living sons. In a true sense, Kathryn gave her life for them to live because her death revealed my wife's incompetent cervix, and that allowed Christopher and Nathan to be safely stitched into the womb.

When Christopher was born in 1996, we wanted to give him a biblical name, so I suggested Luke. And then we could give him the middle name Sky, so he would be Luke Sky Walker. But for some reason, my wife wouldn't agree to that, and George Lucas wanted a nickel every time we used his name.

If you're a parent, then you know how you try out many names but eventually one settles in as the right one, and so we called him Christopher, which means "Christbearer."

His was a perfect pregnancy until two days before the delivery date, when he decided to rotate for a better view and then he was in breech position. But he was born healthy and I remember staring at him, thinking he looked like someone in the family: Was it my dad? Was it my wife's dad? Then, like the mud clearing from a pond that has been disturbed, I realized he looked just like me.

He was as articulate as any adult by the time he was two; he came to Christ at a Billy Graham crusade, and I've always marveled how a man of the twentieth century led a boy who will live in the twenty-first century to Jesus. As I've watched Christopher grow, sometimes I feel as if I look away for a second, and when I look back, he's older, almost a young man, then when I look again he is truly a young man.

Our youngest son was born a year after Jeremy in 2000. We were going to name him Jason and even had some baby things with that name on it. The morning of his delivery date, I was studying in Jeremiah. God says he knew Jeremiah in the womb, and that he was going to give him to the nations. The Hebrew word for "give" can be rendered as *nathan*. In Jeremiah's context it represents a gift from God.

I was certain the Holy Spirit was telling me that we should name the baby Nathan. We were already in the hospital, and there was suddenly a concern that the baby's heart was weakening. The doctors had to get him out of the womb as quickly as possible. Just before they wheeled my wife in for a Caesarean, we prayed and then I told her, "I think God is telling me that we should name him Nathan."

There is no way to describe the grief and pain that comes from missing my sons. I see them a lot; they even live with me on certain weekends. But there is something lost when you do not live with them every day. You miss them running in from school and talking about their day. You miss being with them when a tooth comes out or when they're getting dressed for their first date. You miss just hanging out with them.

Sure, you can hear about it later. You can text and face-time, but it's still not the same. In some ways, it's like someone knocks on your door and says she's come to take your children to college. "But they're only eight and thirteen. I was planning several more years before they left home."

"That's okay," the someone says, "you can see them on holidays."

I have been my sons' father their whole lives, but now I have a document that dictates when I can see them (let me note that my wife allows us lots of extra time). I have to knock on the door to see my sons, when before they were just a few steps down the hall. Now I have to take a legal form to school to prove I have joint custody and that I am their legal guardian.

I may be an ex-husband, but I am not an ex-father.

I remember when they moved out, it grieved me that I didn't know anything about where they were living. I hadn't seen their rooms. Can you understand that? I wanted to see where they were going to sleep, study, and dream. My oldest son walked back to the house a few days after they moved out in order to see if he could do that to come over regularly. My youngest son would arrive pulling a carry-on bag behind him—to me a heart-rending reflection of what we do to children in divorce.

——— ——

I wander through my Zillow dreams, somehow thinking my sons are at a disadvantage living in an apartment. But my friend and spiritual mentor, Steve Pettit reminds me that I do not know where my sons will grow the best spiritually. Only God knows.

Maybe it is in an apartment that they deepen their relationship with Jesus. I hear him, and I understand him, but it is hard to let go. They are my sons and I want to give them the best, but I see my disconnect. Is the best a house to live in or an intimate relationship with Jesus?

Bonhoeffer says no disciple is exempt from carrying the cross he or she is assigned. This means, for instance, we cannot use our children as an excuse to disobey the commands of Jesus. If Jesus says move to this neighborhood, we cannot say, "But Jesus, that's not where I want to raise my kids. I'll move there after they have grown up." We often decide where to live and what to do based on faithless thinking and our own selfish desires. I remember standing in one house, asking God, "How do we know which one of these houses to buy? Which one will be best for raising the boys?" Then, I started playing "Where's Waldo" with God, as if he wouldn't answer my prayer directly and in a way I could easily understand.

——— ——

I've come to hate the house we lost. It was all wrong, and we lost so much. No backyard, no playset for Nathan. No bonus room for Christopher. This is the way I was thinking.

Then, one day Nathan tells me it was his favorite house because he got to spend so much time with me up in the bonus room-turned-apartment. For a second, I feel like I've stopped breathing because suddenly I'm conscious of taking in a huge breath of air, sucking it in as if my lungs had been totally empty. I've been so focused on material provision, when he simply wanted to be with me.

I think about sitting in our idealized California backyard working on my laptop while the boys were swimming, and I can't even remember what was so important that I wasn't in the pool with them. I think about asking a friend, "Since when did spending time with my sons on a Saturday become an inconvenience?"

And now that I do not live with them, I often think about the times I had a chance to do things with them and didn't. I'm like a boxer who carries the scars of every heavyweight fight I've had with guilt and regret. No need to confront me with my failures; I have not forgotten them.

I say, "Well, I've just been concerned about how much you guys have lost through the divorce. I mean, we lost the house."

And Nathan says, "And I lost you."

The boxer starts to cry.

chapter 20

RETRIBUTION

It may surprise you to know that the person I had the
most difficulty forgiving after my divorce was not my wife, but
someone in the legal system who had been entrusted to help me
through such a confusing and emotionally distressing time. This
hurt me in ways that can never be measured. My growing financial crisis was ignored, and I was left horribly vulnerable as we
entered mediation.

Looking back on that time, I have a sense of terrible lost-
ness, unsure of what to do and how to move forward. I was
traveling the treacherous terrain of a divorce system that is
sick with cynicism and fueled by greed and fear. The system is
designed to establish husbands and wives as adversaries, and
it is largely managed by attorneys, of whom many operate as

independent financial franchises with surprisingly little over-sight by the court.

Although I could have tried to draw more support from friends and the church, I trusted a specialist to guide me through the proceedings, and I finished with an emotional sense like this: I hired an experienced protector to walk me down a notoriously dangerous street; yet, when I was pulled into an alley and brutally beaten, my bodyguard simply watched while joking about how much I'd paid for the protection.

I survived the experience, but like a victim of a violent crime, I lost more than material things. I'm left feeling betrayed and broken; I'm shamed and humiliated; I'm completely con-fused and utterly without confidence.

All of this slowly crept into my innermost parts, and I slipped into a deep depression. There was nothing I could do to undo the damage, and every day I bore a heavy burden because of a system designed to create winners and losers.

And this is where Bonhoeffer and I had some intense dis-cussions. I would walk Jasmine around the yard going over and over this teaching, knowing it was true but not wanting to accept it.

Bonhoeffer says, if you want to follow Jesus, then you must give up your right to get even. And he notes that this is another occasion where we decide for or against Jesus. Will you trust God to handle the situation or will you trust your own abili-ties? Do you have faith enough to stand back and watch God handle the situation or do you have to push in with your own vengeance? Bonhoeffer isn't saying you can't protect yourself or stand up for your rights; he is saying the responsibility for how to deal with someone who has wronged you belongs to God.

> Bonhoeffer says, if you want to follow Jesus, then you must give up your right to get even. And he notes that this is another occasion where we decide for or against Jesus.

But here's where I kept stumbling: Would you rather God condemn your enemies or redeem them? Consider the work Jesus must do in us to get us from one side of that question to the other. In my anger, I'm not sure I want God to redeem them. I can give you a Sunday morning rah-rah, "Okay, God, sounds good to me," but in practice, I'm not sure I'm ready for that Kingdom thought.

Okay God, how about this: Redeem them, but hurt them first.

I was struck with this aspect of faith. Do I trust God enough to handle vengeance for me, and would I be satisfied if God said, "Okay, the way I handled that is I redeemed them. They're getting on the same bus as you going to heaven."

God knows the whole truth of every situation and he also knows that our fight is often not with the person in front of us but with the Enemy beyond.

Bonhoeffer says that any thoughts that Jesus doesn't understand how difficult it is to live in a sinful and fallen world are absurd. *Jesus, you just don't understand how hurtful and aggressive others can be. You don't understand the need to pro-tect yourself!*

Really? Doesn't it show the depth of our delusional think-ing that we would say this to a man who, half dead, carried a Roman cross through the streets of Jerusalem, only to have nails driven into his hands and feet before he was hoisted into the air to hang from the cross?

But here's the real Kingdom thought: Jesus is telling us, "I have better things for you to do than to chase after revenge. I want you focused on kingdom work, helping me to bring others into the kingdom. So don't be foolish! Revenge is a job that our Father set aside for himself. Do you really think you can do a better job than God at getting even? Do you really want to get in the way of God when he is handling revenge for you?"

——— ——

Bonhoeffer says the only way we can bear someone else's sin "is by forgiving it in the power of the cross of Christ in which [we] now share." He says forgiving others is the Christlike suffering we are called to bear and this requires another shift in our thinking because it destroys any fantasy that forgiveness is all about "being nice" and "can't we all just get along."

Forgiveness is a bloody work that costs, not only the life of Jesus, but your own life as well: *For if you want to save your own life, you will lose it; but if you lose your life for me and for the gospel, you will save it.* Grace is free but it bloody-well isn't cheap. If every time we sinned, we could hear the clank of hammer to nail through wrist, the devil would have a harder time selling us on his inventory of sin.

It is bearing the sins of others, even when it means suffering and rejection, that creates the distinction between "an ordinary human life and a life committed to Christ," says Bonhoeffer. To echo the apostle Paul, "We can understand someone dying for a person worth dying for, and we can understand how someone good and noble could inspire us to selfless sacrifice," but to forgive others, even when it means suffering and rejection, who could do that but someone compelled by the power of God? (quoted section from Romans 5:7 MSG).

> It is bearing the sins of others, even when it means suffering and rejection, that creates the distinction between "an ordinary human life and a life committed to Christ," says Bonhoeffer.

One day I went to the hospital, thinking I was having a heart attack. I wasn't, but the nurse asked me if there was anyone she should call in case of an emergency. I said, "No one. There's no one you can call." She said, "Do you live alone?" "Yes, I do."

Now there were friends I could have told her to call, but the conversation reflected my sense of isolation and abandonment. They wanted to do some tests, but I skipped them because I didn't feel I had the luxury to spend the money required to cover the co-pay.

The divorce agreement kept me under constant stress and I began to have serious concerns about my ability to work at all. My medical condition has no bearing on the divorce agreement, unless I can convince the court that I have a medical disability. It seems a Catch 22 situation: As long as I'm still on my feet, the court expects me to keep going; once I crash and burn, then the court might consider my bipolar condition.

But any petition before the court means paying more to an attorney, and the monster issue before me is money. I have to keep generating income in order to pay my wife, pay my own bills, and try to build some sort of reserve. If I stop doing that, I am in contempt of court and daily drilling deeper into a financial hole from which I may never recover.

The pressure I was feeling pushed me deeper and deeper into depression. I'd hit difficult days in the past but always knew I would eventually turn the corner around the crisis. But now I'm not certain . . . no, I don't believe I can turn this corner. I don't think I'm going to make it. The slope is too slippery.

Have I reached the point where it is time to quit? I start to wonder if the court would pay attention if I killed myself and left a note explaining why. Maybe it could spark a whole movement to reform the divorce system? Maybe I'm having maudlin, middle school fantasies.

But it is a depressing thought to realize that my family would be better off financially if I were dead instead of alive. Although I would have done this voluntarily, the divorce court required me to keep a life insurance policy on myself with my wife as the beneficiary. But in this post-ERA culture, the same court does not require a wife to keep a life insurance policy on herself with her husband as the beneficiary..

I think about the financial difficulty I will face if my wife dies, and I am left with the boys. I think about the fact that I will have to go to court to reclaim my two sons. I think about keeping up this kind of existence long-term and it just exhausts me. Will there ever be a time when this burden will lift? Am I just burned out and done, becoming one of those people who keeps on breathing but just waiting to die.

I will tell you honestly that I am ready for death. I will welcome the day it comes. I know there is nowhere else to go but to Jesus. I am increasingly certain he is active in my life. "But, hey Jesus, I'm still having trouble seeing the Romans 8:28 in this!" I know he is on the other side of this life on earth. What on earth am I here for wrestles with how much longer must I stay here, Lord?

I am tired and exhausted by life. There are some days that just putting on my socks is a major victory. I once read about a survey where men who'd gone through both clinical depression and cancer were asked, if they had to experience one of the diseases again, which one would they choose? Almost every one of them said they rather go through cancer again than the depression.

When I think of suicide, it is with a detached eye. I want to kill the pain, not necessarily myself. I want to end the exhaustion. And so I find I can hold two disparate thoughts together in my head. I'll end my life tonight, then meet with the boys on Saturday.

Jasmine nudges my arm. I push her away. She keeps nudging my arm. She won't let me stay in bed. She forces me to get up and move, one of the best things you can do in depression.

Is it possible this dog is saving my life? Is it a coincidence that God gave me this specific dog, who won't take no for an answer?

I take her for a walk and hear a quick, uneven succession of thuds back by the carport. We walk in that direction and I see that three turkey vultures are sitting on the fence staring at me with malicious intent. I wonder what has brought them closer to the house; what dead carcass attracts them. I wonder if that carcass is me.

I've been in the same clothes for a week. I'm not sure what day it is. I thought I took my medication yesterday, but when I look at my pill box, I realize I ran out three days ago. It seems like such an effort to count out the pills again.

Through my lethargic mind, I begin to see that I have romanticized my disease. My doctor told me it was the kind of thing where people just dropped out and disappeared. I thought she meant someone who dropped out of the rat race and sought a simpler life.

But I realize now she meant that, if I was not careful, then little by little I could drop right out of life. And in a case like mine, with no assets and no spouse, I could slip right into subsistence living. It is only now that I realize I have a major disease, and that I have to handle this differently. But it also underscores my fears because—what is to become of me?

My doctor tells me I'm not managing my disease well. I'd never thought of it that way but I understand now. But I'm also so very, very tired. I think I'm ready to give up. I consider the reasons to keep going and I can only come up with two: my sons.

I don't mean this in a superficial, sappy way. I mean this as a man who has lost so much and now realizes that so very little of it really mattered in the face of eternity. What does a house compare to my two sons?

I find so many things don't mean as much as they used to, and I think about what there is left in life that I really want. I have no need for possessions and I'm slowly giving away anything I don't actually use. I'm content without a lot of money. I wanted to write one book that would have an impact but does that really matter? If I'm near the end, then relationships are all that matter. I can't really think of anything I want apart from providing for my sons and spending time with them.

I think about Bonhoeffer saying that grace is free but it will cost us everything, and I see his point as I look at how Jesus has led me down narrower paths into places where I was forced to choose for or against him. I ended up in places I never expected. He asked, "Will you still follow me regardless of what you're paid?" "Will you still follow me, even if you're not paid?" Will you still follow me, even if you don't get credit?" "Will you still follow me, even if someone else gets the credit?" "Will you still follow me, even if no one seems to care what you're doing?" "Will you still follow me, even if no one says thanks?"

Like a surgeon using a scalpel, Jesus cuts away anything that dilutes the purity of our motives for following him. But we must choose each time whether or not to go forward.

I'm letting things go. Although I come in through the door of depression, I see there is nothing I need to do to make my life complete. I am complete in Christ. I don't need the extra, for instance, the last dying dream of being a great writer.

I am a man who was born and lived and served God in the midst of my many, many flaws, and I will be with him in heaven because Jesus wrapped me in his righteousness and I trusted that to be true.

"The fact that Jesus Christ died is more important than the fact that I shall die, and the fact that Jesus Christ rose from the dead is the sole ground of my hope that I, too, shall be raised on the Last Day," says Bonhoeffer. "Our salvation is 'external to ourselves.' I find no salvation in my life history, but only in the history of Jesus Christ. Only he who allows himself to be found in Jesus Christ, in his incarnation, his cross, and his resurrection, is with God and God with him."

My life story provides no salvation. It doesn't matter who I've been or what I've done or how nice of a guy I tried to be. What matters is the work of Jesus Christ and my willingness to submit to him.

Shortly after Jesus fed the five thousand, the disciples realized they'd forgotten to bring food for themselves on their journey across the Sea of Galilee. In essence, they began to wonder how they would eat, and Jesus looked at them and said, "Why are you discussing among yourselves about not having any bread? What little faith you have! Don't you understand yet? Don't you remember when I broke the five loaves for the five thousand men? How many baskets did you fill? And what about the seven loaves for the four thousand men? How many baskets did you fill?" (Matthew 16:8-10 TEV).

> "Our salvation is 'external to ourselves.'
> I find no salvation in my life history, but
> only in the history of Jesus Christ. Only he
> who allows himself to be found in Jesus
> Christ, in his incarnation, his cross, and his
> resurrection, is with God and God with him."
> —BONHOEFFER

Of more significance than forgetting bread for the day, they had forgotten the miracles of Jesus performed right before their eyes. They had lowered their eyes from the Kingdom and begun to see only what was right in front of them.

So had I. Without a doubt, so had I.

I see now that I have what I need. For instance, I do not need a house pulled from my Zillow dreams. The truth is, I have a house, provided by God through the Moffitts. It has a yard, some elbow room, and a place my sons and I can call home. I am a steward, but that is all any of us are if we look into Kingdom reality.

In God's Kingdom economy, he provides for us in his own way: rather than giving me money to pay for a place to live, he provides for us through the gracious generosity of the Moffitts, and I have no doubt he is providing for them in the other unique, unexpected ways of his Kingdom economy.

And this is where I died, right here. As Paul says, "It is no longer I who live, but it is Christ who lives in me. This life that I live now, I live by faith in the Son of God, who loved me and gave his life for me" (Galatians 2:19-2o TEV).

As I'm thinking this, I hear a commotion on the roof. I step out onto the deck and the vultures are huddled around the chimney, looking like devilish mischief-makers. I stare at them for a moment, and then I quietly say, "There's nothing here for you today. It is true I have died but I am also alive in Christ. If you smell death, it is because Jesus has killed off my delusions and my faulty belief that I could make myself into a nice guy. But these things are at the feet of Jesus, and they're not for you. So please leave, you have no right to torment me."

They simply stared back at me, one finally spitting out an odd squawk. I have not seen the vultures since this conversation.

I go back inside and think about Bonhoeffer saying, "Thus it begins. The cross is not the terrible end to an otherwise God fearing and happy life, but it meets us at the beginning of our communion with Christ. When Christ calls a man, he bids him come and die."

chapter 21

FRESH MERCIES EACH MORNING

When I left LifeWay on faith, I told one of my bosses that I wanted to engage an exceptional faith. Naively, I said, "I want to pray for the money I need, and then walk to the mailbox the next day and find a check for exactly the amount I need." It was a romanticized view of living by faith.

Shortly after the divorce, someone asked me what I did for a living. Having no job, and always one for gallows humor, I said, "I live on faith, and every fear I ever had about doing that has come true."

Walking by faith is exhausting until we transition into trust, and I know that is why I stopped short along the way. But the truth is, we step out of our fears by stepping forward in faith.

With each step, we learn, like Abraham, that the promise does not depend on what represents our Isaac, but on God alone. Jesus is teaching me about a ruthless love that gives no quarter to an anemic, nice-guy Christianity. He is my king and he will take what he must take and demand what he must demand in order to prepare me for the Kingdom of Heaven.

> "When Christ calls a man,
> he bids him come and die."
> —BONHOEFFER

Almost every day Jasmine and I walk through a neighborhood populated by mansions worth about a million dollars. I see the high-end of the American dream, including boats and BMWs and designer furniture. And, deep at the end of the neighborhood, Jasmine and I find our God-loaned simple farmhouse with its uneven floors and cracked walls and vulture-free barn, and I know I'm home because I've living where God wants me to live.

And the grace of God that surrounds this home is a reminder to me that the place Jesus prepares for me will be greater than any of the mansions next to me. If, in the future, God blesses me financially, I know I'll use that money far differently than I would have three years ago. And I'm grateful he pushed me hard into Kingdom thinking so I can spend the last years of my life focused on the things that are truly—and eternally—important.

As that great theologian, Frodo, says, "How do you pick up the threads of an old life? How do you go on, when in your heart you begin to understand . . . there is no going back?"

Every day Jesus calls us to a choice: Will we chose for him or against him? Here's the thing about our choices: Bonhoeffer notes that Levi could have stayed at his post when Jesus called him to follow and Jesus would have been a part of Levi's life. But Jesus never would have been the Lord of Levi's whole life.

Is it that we don't want to enter into Kingdom maturity, or is it that we don't believe God can make us mature?

DIETRICH BONHOEFFER

Dietrich Bonhoeffer's life was one of risk, where he faced constant choices that required him to take a stand, often putting everything he had—even his life—on the line for what he believed. It's easy to marvel at the way he faced off against Adolf Hitler and the Nazi regime, but in his books, such as "The Cost of Discipleship," Bonhoeffer teaches that a life of such extraordinary risk is the *expectation*, not the exception, for any disciple of Jesus.

To me, what is appealing about the Bonhoeffer is his authenticity. He walked steadily toward an uncompromising faith in Jesus and he did it in the difficult and dangerous reality of life, where obeying the commands of Christ can often be heart-wrenching and costly. Perhaps because he was thrust so quickly and so young into life or death matters, Bonhoeffer did not play games with pastoral piety or write from an ivory tower.

Too young to be ordained when he first graduated from seminary, Bonhoeffer continued his theological studies at Union Theological Seminary in New York City, and for a brief time taught Sunday school at Abyssinian Baptist Church in Harlem, New York. There Adam Clayton Powell, Sr. preached a social gospel that would significantly influence the Civil Rights movement in the United States.

It was Powell who first used the term "cheap grace" to describe the way the church compromises the gospel when it down-plays the cross and repentance in order to sell an easy discipleship that requires little commitment and suggests there is a pain-free path into heaven. The take-away for Bonhoeffer was that, to echo his own words, his religious phraseology quickly transformed into real Christian action. For such a time as this, God sent him back to Germany.

It was a little over a year after Bonhoeffer was ordained as a Lutheran pastor that the Nazis came to power on January 30, 1933. Bonhoeffer, still only twenty-six-years-old, delivered a radio address two days later, where he warned the German people that they were being seduced by the Führer and that their worship of him would lead to idolatry. His broadcast was cut off in mid-sentence.

The young pastor watched in dismay as the state-sponsored church of Germany compromised with Hitler and so he became a founding member of the Confessing Church, which was comprised of congregations independent of government sponsorship. A gifted theologian, Bonhoeffer might have taught in any number of professorships or pastorates, but his opposition to Adolf Hitler closed the door to those opportunities. Instead, he began teaching in less formal settings, such as the unofficial Finkenwalde Seminary.

It was at Finkenwalde that Bonhoeffer began writing *The Cost of Discipleship*, publishing the manuscript in 1937, about the same time the Gestapo shut down the seminary and arrested many of its students. In 1938 Bonhoeffer published *Life Together*, a book that describes how to live in Christian community.

In 1939 Bonhoeffer returned to Union Theological Seminary in New York City to teach, but almost immediately regretted his decision, believing he would have no right to participate in the reconstruction of Christian life in Germany after the war if he wasn't there to share in the hardships of the German people during the war.

Returning to Germany, Bonhoeffer joined the *Abwehr*, a branch of Germany's military intelligence, but also the center for the resistance movement in Germany. For instance, the *Abwehr* worked to undermine Nazi policy toward the Jews and Bonhoeffer also used his position as cover as he traveled and spoke, something he would not otherwise be allowed to do.

In April 1943, Bonhoeffer was arrested and imprisoned in Tegel military prison while awaiting trial. He continued his ministry in prison, including writing letters and papers that became a book published posthumously.

It wasn't until the July 20 Plot ("Valkyrie") that Bonhoeffer's involvement was discovered by the Gestapo. His death was ordered by Adolf Hitler and on April 8, 1945, Bonhoeffer was executed by hanging at Flossenbürg concentration camp—a mere three weeks before Hitler committed suicide as the Allies swept into Berlin. Bonhoeffer's parents, Karl and Paula, saw two sons and two sons-in-law executed during World War II for their part in the German Resistance.

Bonhoeffer died in the same way he lived, focused exclusively on Christ and humbly submitting to the ultimate cost of discipleship. Offered an opportunity to escape, he declined, not wanting to put his family in danger. He was led to the gallows after concluding a Sunday morning service, saying: "This is the end—for me the beginning of life."

He has become one of the most influential theological voices of the twentieth century and *The Cost of Discipleship* is considered a classic in ecclesiological literature. Many of its concepts are now deeply ingrained in modern Protestant thought and practice.

If you'd like to read more about Bonhoeffer, this excellent biography is available: *Bonhoeffer: Pastor, Martyr, Prophet, Spy*, by Eric Metaxas (Thomas Nelson, 2010).

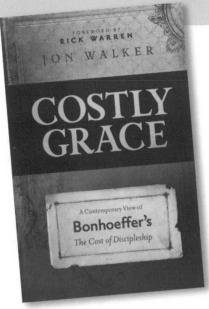